A great testament of strength and perseveran(
spirit and encourage you to keep going under

Cancer R.I.P. is brilliant! As a stem cell transplant patient and cancer survivor, I found that *Cancer R.I.P.* gripped me, made me laugh, and made me cry again. Steve stole me from the present and took me back to my own treatments. Steve forced me to look at everything I had hidden from myself. And then he made me laugh and cry again. I learned so much about myself.

—GLORIA ARONSON
FELLOW CANCER SURVIVOR

Tremendous story. A testimony to perseverance.

—VINCENT BEAUDOIN
CONFIDANT

In *Cancer R.I.P.*, Steve Kelley does what he does best...face any challenge head on and with humor! Steve made his cancer "a thing" called She so that the reader could identify with the illness. *Cancer R.I.P.* is a must-read if you want to find courage and humor when you are really frightened by an illness.

—JOSEPH FEASTER
FELLOW CANCER SURVIVOR

Cancer R.I.P. is an inspiring firsthand story of Steve's journey to overcome a deadly cancer diagnosis. Steve has a unique ability to take a deadly diagnosis head on with his optimism, strength, and unique perspective. His story will bring up all of your emotions. He will even have you laughing when you would least expect it. You will be cheering Steve on, smiling and believing in the power of a positive mindset and a great support system.

—SERENA FINOCCHIO
YOGA INSTRUCTOR

As physicians focused on science and clinical performance, we often do not get the opportunity to understand the effect illness has on the patient's mind and soul. Steve Kelley's *Cancer R.I.P.* is an invaluable window for all physicians to see how one extraordinary patient personally perceives his cancer and the emotional toll of our treatments on him. Written with wit, wisdom, and thoroughly entertaining prose, *Cancer R.I.P.* is a beautiful lesson to both patient and physician.

—YAKOV KOGAN
M.D.

When I first met Steve Kelley, he was anticipating his brain surgery but spoke of it as if it were knee surgery. The guy is focused on being positive in all aspects of his life. When my wife was undergoing cancer treatments at Dana-Farber, the medical professionals stressed keeping a positive attitude and how that influenced results. Steve Kelley's experiences—as captured in his new book—demonstrate that. Steve Kelley is just about the most positive-thinking person I have ever met. His new book on his experiences with brain cancer is a great read for all regardless of one's experience or inexperience with cancer.

— JAMES M. LEWIS
ESQUIRE & FELLOW MOUNTAIN BIKER
LEWIS & SULLIVAN, P.C.

Steve Kelley's remarkable recovery from inoperable brain cancer and subsequent stem cell transplant is laid out in riveting detail in *Cancer R.I.P.* with every chapter giving advice on fighting the demon. From the get-go Steve engages with the enemy on a first-name basis, like two gladiators in an arena. With an incredible medical team behind him, his good humor and resolutely positive mindset at every stage belie the seriousness of his situation. Ultimately, his amazing return to daily life is testament to his fighting spirit. With superb writing skills, Steve turns a heavy subject into a must-read. Cancer is no thrill but Steve's lessons are invaluable.

—ROBERT LUCKOCK
JOURNALIST

Cancer R.I.P. rocks! I laughed so hard, got emotional, and had lots of "ah-ha!" moments. Talk about the power of perspective and adjusting. Wow! Steve's perspective and attitude is remarkable, inspiring, and can be applied to any of life's battles. Steve reminds us throughout the book of how powerful the mind is, and that the fight begins and ends with our minds. Thank you for this gem of a book, Steve!

—VANESSA LUNDY
INSPIRED FRIEND

Steve Kelley's *Cancer R.I.P.* chronicles with warmth, humor, and combative insight the death blow he gave to cancer, and provides a road map for others to succeed as he did. Cancer lacked the strength to defeat Steve Kelley. Steve's *Cancer R.I.P.* shows that a lifetime of living gave him the strength to battle cancer and win the battle.

—BOB MENDILLO
ATTORNEY & WRITER
STOUGHTON, MA

Cancer R.I.P. tells the story of my best friend and mountain biking partner's battle with brain cancer. In the very first weeks of battle, brain cancer transformed my high-energy amigo into a shadow of himself who could barely remember my name or find his way home from the trails. Cancer won that early battle, but cancer has lost the war to Steve's medical team, dedicated friends, and personal tenacity. Together we transformed cancer into a low-energy, impotent shadow of a disease, who can barely raise her head or remember Steve's name.

—LUIS TUEME
Steve's Best Friend

Wow, Steve! Thank you for writing this powerful book. I watched Steve deal with cancer firsthand and was inspired by his determination and positive attitude. *Cancer R.I.P.* will touch your heart. Be prepared to laugh and cry as you read Steve's story.

—RABBI HENRY M. MORSE
Sha'ar Hashamayim Stoughton

Steve Kelley's writing is gripping, surprising, chilling at times. And then, suddenly your feelings are in control, ready for anything, amazing!

—LINDA OSTRANDER PH.D.
Author of eight books,
Composer, Pianist, & Professor

Cancer R.I.P. is an authentic account of Steve's determination to rid himself of cancer. Steve stares down his disease with the tenacity of a prize fighter while using optimism and humor to share his experiences with the reader.

—DAVID RUDNICK
Attorney, Entrepreneur,
& Mountain Biker

Steve has the amazing talent of taking a life-threatening personal situation and making it a source of solace and hope for us all. His down-to-earth writing lets you inside his head while he's battling to get cancer out. This truly is an inspirational read.

—DAVID WLUKA
Close Friend

In an instant you had my attention. After a moment, you had more than my attention.

—PAUL WOOD
Fellow Writer

STEVE KELLEY

CANCER R.I.P.

The Ultimate Fight

Edited by Carol McAdoo Rehme

One Stop
PUBLISHING

One Stop Publishing Group, LLC | www.OneStopPublishing.com

STOUGHTON MASSACHUSETTS

Cancer R.I.P.: The Ultimate Fight

Steve Kelley

© 2021 by Steve Kelley

Freedom Press Consulting

Publisher: One Stop Publishing
             PO Box 474
             Stoughton, MA 02072
             Onestoppublishing.com

ISBN: 978-0-578-84704-7

DEDICATION

To all the wonderful people who helped me through the
cancer journey—most especially my beautiful wife, Susan,
my sons, Dave and Phil, my daughters-in-law, Jess and
Rory, my stepson, Dave, and his wife, Michelle, my Stinky
Brats, and my biking buddies.

TABLE OF CONTENTS

FOREWORD

Taking care of people with brain cancer has been my greatest honor and privilege. Every day, I witness the strength of my patients and their loved ones as they battle against this vicious, invasive beast. Over the years, my concept of life and its meaning has changed. I have learned so much from my patients, not just about brain cancer, but about life itself. And so, when Steve approached me to pen a few words and contribute a sketch, I was incredibly touched.

Cancer is one of the biggest and worst fears of most human beings. But what is unique to brain cancers and CNS lymphoma is the impact of cancer on the loss of self. Losing the ability to talk, think, or walk—the essence of an individual's humanness, which we often take for granted—is extremely humbling. In *Cancer R.I.P.*, Steve candidly discloses his vulnerabilities as he braves through the disease and treatments.

Writing a book, particularly about your experience, can be challenging, yet Steve expresses himself effectively and, importantly, brings humor into the conversation about the most difficult time of his life. His writing is fluid, and he swiftly takes you with him through his voyage across the tempestuous sea of brain cancer, not just staying afloat but thriving until he reaches land.

FOREWORD

You hear his cries and feel his anxiety in the tight enclosure of the MRI machine. You experience how he gets lost while driving, and you hope he makes it home okay—only to be confronted further with the diagnosis of cancer. When he is informed he has brain cancer, you feel the jolt.

As you journey with him, Steve points out how each experience informed his life with lessons. He reveals his deepest secrets and eloquently exposes the fragile nature of the human mind and body. Steve has a unique way of humanizing cancer and the emotions associated with it. This distinctive capability allowed for his healing—mental, physical, and spiritual. He describes how acknowledging one's emotions is key to acceptance in order to climb on the not-so-fast track to recovery. He utilizes kindness and humor as his tools to cope with his horrors.

I am reminded of his positive attitude during chemotherapy and, in particular, his smiling face while he endured the rigorous effects of stem cell transplant. In fact, I don't think I have ever seen Steve without a smile on his face. He truly embodies what it means to be an eternal optimist.

You will cry and laugh as you read *Cancer R.I.P.* and learn about the repercussions of brain cancer, the relevance of time, and, finally, how to heal. This book is a source of inspiration worth reading and then rereading.

—LAKSHMI NAYAK, M.D.
Assistant Professor of Neurology, Harvard Medical School
Director, Center for CNS Lymphoma,
Dana-Farber Cancer Institute

Disclaimer: The contents of this book are the opinions of the author and do not represent the opinion or perception of Dr. Lakshmi Nayak or Dana-Farber Cancer Institute.

Chapter 1

MY SECRET VISITOR

*Secrets are dark things. They don't exist in the light.
They glow faintly in forgotten corners,
in mysterious mind nooks,
in lost memory maps.
Secrets are the shadows of the soul.*
— SUKANYA VENKATRAGHAVAN

Chapter 1

I don't know why *She* came or when *She* started stalking me.

My first glimpse of her was fleeting, barely a shadow over my shoulder. *She* wasn't ugly, but *She* wasn't pretty, either. *She* was formless. Not fat, not skinny; not black, not white. Yet, somehow, I knew my stalker was female.

She didn't draw much attention in the beginning. That would change. I didn't have to like her and *She* didn't care. *She* was determined to be in my life. I couldn't remember when we first met or how *She* found me.

I woke up one day and *She* was with me, attached. No matter how hard I tried to shake her off, *She* was determined to stay. *She* was, in point of fact, destined to be my companion for life.

I found out her first secrets on June 1, 2018, a day I recall vividly … although those that followed are a blur. *She* stomped in with heavy footsteps, impatiently banging her heels. When *She* waved the key in front of me and thumbed her nose, I thought I heard her whisper, "I got you, you bastard! I'm in."

I froze. I didn't know what to do.

Until then, *She* had been sneaking around, mostly unnoticed. Where was *She* from? Was *She* local? How did *She* get in? Somewhere down the hall? Through the cellar? *She* held the answer to so many secrets.

I should have locked the damn door!

MY SECRET VISITOR

Inside each of us is a house with great architecture: lots of doors, entries with locks needing keys. Rooms connected by a maze of intricate hallways. Some we see, some are hidden away, unknown.

In my internal house, I'm sure you'd never find your way without a map. You couldn't enter without a key, which begs the questions: How did *She* get inside? How did *She* procure a key? A map? Eerie thoughts roamed my mind. Was *She* from the future sneaking back to the present to toy with me? Or was *She* the adventurer inside me, leaping forward to see ahead and then come back to warn me?

Or, was *She* evil? Did *She* come to hurt me by delivering a selfish, angry beating because .... friend or foe, it didn't matter what I thought. *She* came onto my stage like a bad actor in a high-school play, who shouts her important-to-her lines too loudly.

I AM cancer! You WILL pay attention to me!

Lessons Learned

- *She* was in my brain, attacking my thinking, my memory, and my body.
- Cancer mounts a relentless siege on its victims.
- Cancer irrevocably alters your life.

Questions Begging Answers

- I'm lousy at being unhealthy. Do I have what it takes to get through this?
- What *does* it take to get through this?
- Will this alter my life permanently?
- What does my future hold?

Chapter 2

FACE-OFF WITH FEAR

Do not go gentle into that good night,
Old age should burn and rave at close of day.
Rage, rage against the dying of the light.
— DYLAN THOMAS

*Y*ahoo!

That's my rallying call when I ride my mountain bike to capture a hill or win a tag-football game on a Sunday or knock in a couple of runs during a weekend softball game.

Since 1980, I have played tag football in a father-son league. My friend Bob and I considered ourselves mentors. We've been most proud of the neighborhood kids, the troubled ones we saved. The kids knew we played every Sunday. If they wanted to join us, they couldn't drink or stay out nearly as late on Saturdays.

We also gave them little pieces of advice, advice they could carry a lifetime: "Hey, Johnny, give your mom a call after the game." "Hey, Healy, ease up. It's only a game."

We were very competitive. With or without referees, games almost always came down to the last play. Regardless of the winner, we told 'em, "Win by twenty or shut the hell up!"

Meaning, if you think you're so good, the game wouldn't have been close and we wouldn't be having these arguments. Local politicians could have done themselves a favor by attending one of our games to learn the same lesson.

After each game, we insisted, "Shake hands. Go home. Lick your wounds and get ready to play another game."

No crying, period!

Sports helped keep me in shape, the kind of shape necessary for the type of work I did, and the kind of playing I've described here.

Roofing and myriads of other physical chores were a constant in my days. Shoveling and plowing during wintertime. Shifting and lifting sand, salt, furniture, shingles .... You name it and I moved it.

I was passionate about sports and the camaraderie of my friends. Slow-pitch softball was a favorite. I pitched high-arc and practiced in batting cages before games.

Then, in a quirky pick-up game, I injured my shoulder.

Timeline: 2003

It happened when I slid into second base, stretching a single into a double—baseball jargon for pushing the envelope to get more out of a small hit than it deserves. The action tore my supraspinatus, typically called a rotator cuff, one of the muscles in your shoulder that allows you to lift your arm.

Afterward, when my brain sent the signal to reach and I stretched upward to obey, nothing happened. Zilch. My arm wouldn't move. When I twisted or attempted to raise my arm quickly without thinking, a jolt of pain shot through me. It wasn't a little bump-into-the-door-of-your-car pain, rather a slam-your-fingers-in-the-door pain. A penetrating stab of startling, eye-opening, screaming pain.

I *had* to get my shoulder fixed to halt the hurt. To be able to lift ladders, to put food in the refrigerator, to lift my two-year-old twin grandchildren in the air. Delighted that my shoulder could be surgically repaired, I readily accepted the operation. And the MRI.

Chapter 2

The MRI would allow Dr. James Karlson, a renowned ortho-
pedic surgeon, to see the exact area of the muscle tear and to know
better how to repair the shoulder.

My son Dave drove me to the hospital. We found our way to the
imaging section of the hospital, handled the intake forms for insurance, and waited in the sitting room.

The space was outfitted with large chairs, a couple of coffee
tables piled with magazines, and several abstract paintings on the
walls, the kind of paintings sophisticated people think are marvelous. I'm not sophisticated. In the construction world where I dwell,
we call splashed paint a mistake that happens when you trip over
something.

From the beginning of the MRI intake process I was uncomfortable, and not by the artwork. The technician was a smart aleck
who smugly described the procedure as routine and overstated the
number of people who sail through it.

Before actually climbing inside the monster, but after Mr. Smart
Aleck's intake spiel, I encountered another unsettling moment.
Street clothes, he announced, weren't allowed. No zippers or metal.
A penny might lurk in the lint of your pocket. A tiny metal frag-
ment like a staple might become a projectile. Or so said Mr. Smart
Aleck. (I still don't know if it's true.)

Does this machine sound harmless to you?

After answering tedious questions about implants, pacemak-
ers, shunts, or possible plates and screws from accidents or previous
operations, you are led to a changing room/waiting area. You are
given—and told to don—a bleached and partly worn-through bed

sheet with strings. You can try to tie them, but the limp ribbons don't hold.

For me, it meant exposing my less-than-calendar-caliber body. Okay, I was fat. If you are going in one of these machines, a beer belly and pleasantly plump physique don't cut it. My broad construction shoulders with years of built-up muscle were a hindrance, not a help.

I don't want to gloss over giving up your clothes. *Really?* If you want to make someone feel self-conscious and vulnerable, just ask him to peel off his duds. Essentially, you are entering what looks like a giant front-loading, five-ton washing machine wearing only your skivvies.

Does that sound like fun to you?

Mr. Smart Aleck reminded me that people breeze right through MRIs. "I've done hundreds of these scans. Don't worry."

Easy for him to say ... from his perspective *outside* the machine ... situated comfortably in the control room.

He was not convincing. I didn't trust him. I wasn't falling in love with this guy at all. He amplified to a fault what I had learned about medical people building a shell around themselves.

My very real concerns waved casually aside, Mr. Smart Aleck hustled me into the MRI room.

I contemplated the contraption: a platform bed mounted on a conveyor belt that glides bumpily into a tube, which creates a magnetic field. Radio signals from the magnetic field create the images needed to view the growth (cancer) in tissue or the damage to muscle, bones, ligaments.

The tube opening wasn't much larger than me. It looked like a casket.

"Mr. Kelley, just climb up and lie down."

The platform was high enough that I needed a short jump to get onto it. I couldn't decide whether to straddle it like a horse or ask for a step stool. With my shoulder hurt, I couldn't easily maneuver myself onto the platform, and I didn't want to climb onto the platform on my knees and spin around. Aggravated, I turned, reached behind using my strong arm, and awkwardly lifted myself onto the edge of the platform. I lay face up, lifting my head to look into the machine I was about to enter.

"No, not that way, Mr. Kelley. Backwards, head first."

"Backwards? Wait!" I held up my good hand signaling to stop. "That's not what I want. I'd like to face the machine as I go into it —so I can see what's happening."

Smart Aleck shook his head. "That's not how it's done, Mr. Kelley."

Are you kidding me? I thought as I procrastinated, shifting side-to-side, trying not to aggravate my injury.

"Mr. Kelley, we are on a schedule. *Please* ...."

Reluctantly, I spun around and lay on my back. I closed my eyes and tried to calm down, but my mind raced like I was free-falling from a cliff. As I lay half-naked, mind scrambling, he placed a rubber, bulb-shaped device in my hand.

"Use this to call me. Squeeze it and I'll stop the machine." His eyes narrowed. "But it will take us longer to finish if you do."

The technician engaged the scanner, and the platform slid into the hungry mouth of the MRI. As I rolled backward, my shoulders unexpectedly squished against the tight sides of the tube. With my face less than six inches from the ceiling, the MRI devoured me.

My head was locked into a rigid frame. I could only see the mask he'd placed on my face because its white frame blocked my vision. Nor could I see outside the plastic covered walls of the machine. The world shrank and closed around me.

I froze.

Get me OUT!

Panic crept into the machine with me. I squeezed the rubber bulb and yelled, "Stop!"

A speaker crackled as Mr. Smart Aleck insisted, "Mr. Kelley, we really shouldn't stop. We are on a tight schedule."

My brain was ready to check out. My breath came hard and fast. My heart raced. The scan was vital, I knew, so I tried harder to distract myself to get through the procedure.

I thought about Dave waiting outside the room, a mere fifty yards or so away. *Here I am in crisis mode and he doesn't know what is happening.*

I thought about Mr. Smart Aleck with his futile attempts to prepare me—which hadn't prepared me at all.

I forced myself to be calm—until the platform began to move backward.

"Stop!" I yelled again. I grimaced and gritted my teeth.

Mr. Smart Aleck pretended to care, pretended everything was normal, but it wasn't.

He doesn't let on that he's seen lots of patients fall apart right before his eyes. He knows, but he doesn't share.

That wouldn't advance his goal: Get you in, get you out. Get on to the next patient.

It's a business.

I was hard on Mr. Smart Aleck, Mr. All-Business. He wouldn't appreciate my view. He'd had time to acclimate, was making good money performing his job. The MRI didn't scare him a whit. He had control.

I didn't.

Sense of control is a major factor in our lives. Whether I *should* feel scared or not wasn't the point. I didn't have control and I was scared to death.

I would've been even more frightened back then had I known that fifteen years later I'd have a brain tumor the size of an avocado— necessitating a nasty repeat of this procedure so my doctors could devise a plan for me to live.

In the moment, however, all I cared about was handling my fear. And watching my ego shredded by a machine and a cocky attendant whose empathy had been pitted against his desire to earn a good livelihood.

I got the sense he didn't care at all. I wasn't right, but I wasn't wrong, either.

Mr. All-Business didn't care. He had to do—I don't know, he didn't say—maybe twelve, maybe twenty scans each day. All he wanted was my images. All I needed were the images. So I stayed. Despite my growing fear and resentment.

I was truly scared by then, and I didn't like being that scared. I was used to conquering fear. I was the go-to guy. I was the fixer. That's why my customers hired me. That's why my crew relied on me to keep them safe and provide a livelihood.

Yet here I was, using every last shred of willpower to hang on, to outlast the beast.

The tech attempted one last time to assert control and move me into position. He adjusted the platform for different angles of imagery. I felt like I was on an amusement park ride without the fun—left only with the terror.

What am I scared of?

Remember the space shuttle that blew up? I do. Remember the bridge that fell apart, killing the people under it? I do. I don't trust people. I don't accept that things will work out when I lower my defenses. I don't trust that nothing will go wrong in a machine designed by someone I don't know and who doesn't care about me, who doesn't know me.

Like fog burned off in the morning sun, self-awareness and a growing clarity came to me. I realized I didn't trust the *person* operating the MRI. I thought he didn't care enough about me to protect me in an emergency.

Me? I wasn't that important to him.

I felt that if I couldn't somehow bring extraordinary value to him, he wouldn't look out for me. The dark side of *me* caused my fear.

The machine started. Waves pulsated against my body. Signals alternated with chirping sounds similar to a fire alarm. In rapid succession, the scanner made screeching, rhythmic noises like a million birds let loose from a cage to careen through the sky above my head. It periodically jolted up and down with very small movements that were multiplied to enormous ones in my brain.

My thoughts flickered like the lights in a disco hall. I wasn't being rational. I knew it as much as I knew Dr. Karlson needed the scan.

I squeezed the bulb again and screamed, "Get me out of here! Now!"

Smart Aleck disgustedly shut down the MRI and rolled me out from the beast. I jumped off the bed, scrambling for balance.

I had failed the test.

Yet this event was more than a failure. It was a life-altering, machine-induced crisis that flayed my confidence. In those short, sweaty, anxiety-filled, intensely panicked moments, I convinced myself I'd rather die than continue.

The technician was insulted. I didn't care.

I was pissed, angry with the guy for not warning me. The guy who had glossed over and pooh-poohed what I found out afterward is a common, intensely claustrophobic reaction. I was angry at him, angry at medicine, angry at the whole medical community for downplaying the procedure.

I felt shamed and needed to throw blame wherever I could. The frightening experience exposed a vulnerability I didn't know I had, so I promised myself I would *never* go through that again.

Well, that promise would come back to bite me.

For the first time in my life I fully understood other people's crazy fears. You know, those long words like arachnophobia (fear of spiders), ophidiophobia (snakes), aerophobia (flying), autophobia (being alone), hemophobia (blood), and so many others that scare the bejesus out of people.

Until then, I had no idea I was claustrophobic. Throughout my life, I had been in multiple elevators and tight quarters, even momentarily trapped under a porch I was repairing—and I was always okay. The fear and anxiety that consumed me in the mouth of that beast completely took me by surprise.

It was devastating. I was embarrassed in front of my son, who had brought me to the appointment. And I embarrassed *me*.

Fortunately, Dr. Karlson was battle-tested and proved it. He performed my surgery, despite the lack of images, and it was a success.

Life, I would discover, doesn't play by my rules. I would have to face down many more MRIs.

Lessons Learned

- An active, healthy lifestyle does not preclude occasional health interruptions.

- I'm claustrophobic in MRI machines. Others endure fears, too.

Questions Begging Answers

- Is self-induced stress controllable?

- Can I overcome my fear of MRIs?

- Might I overcome my fear and teach others how to do the same?

- Could that be my incentive, a bigger-picture goal to help me through?

Chapter 3

BAKED TO A CRISP ON A HOT ROOF

*God, it was hot! Forget about
frying an egg on the sidewalk;
this kind of heat would fry an egg
inside the chicken.*
— RACHEL CAINE

Timeline: 2014

D espite my vow—*never again!*—eleven years later an opportunity arose that gave me a shot at redeeming myself, salvaging my ego ... making peace with those damn MRIs once and for all.

Disregarding the scorching 120° heat atop the flat roof we were on (95° on the ground), my roofing crew labored feverishly to finish. As I scanned my workers, clearly visible heat waves distorted my view at the far end of the roof, three hundred feet away. The black rubber on the flat roof had intensified the heat and fried our faces for hours with no shade, no respite from the August day.

To protect my sun-scorched head, I wore a white cloth draped over my neck, tucked under my company-issued baseball hat. I soaked the cloth in water every half hour to cool me down, a simple trick I'd adopted after years of sweat-filled roofing.

With a big weekend storm in the forecast, the crew and I, along with my grandchildren Cam and Chloe, hustled through several days to get the job watertight.

At age sixty, I was training my teenaged grandkids in the family business. I wanted them to learn toughness and how to work through everything: heat, big jobs, stress. My grandkids watched me, much like all kids watch their parents.

The hypocrisy of my own parents preaching one thing while doing the opposite during my childhood was not an example I wanted to emulate. My sons and I worked hard in our roofing business; I wanted Cam and Chloe to experience that same toughness. They would need it in life; all of us need it.

My son Phil—who had been enrolled in my toughness school for forty of his forty-five years since I adopted him at age five—worked alongside me. He was on board with toughening up Cam and Chloe, though his wife, Jess, was less than excited but still supportive. Roofs are not the safest places to be; she had good reason to be skeptical.

With my focus squarely on the safety of our fifteen-person crew and my grandchildren, I didn't drink enough water. Big mistake. Hydration is key when temperatures are over 100°. I knew that. No excuse. In the intense heat I dried up like a prune. I should have *pushed* more water into my system.

When I came down from the roof, Phil glanced at me, confused and startled.

"What's wrong with your eye, Dad?"

"What do you mean?"

He tilted his head at me. "You look crazily cross-eyed."

I didn't know how I looked, but I noticed my peripheral sightline was skewed with double vision when I looked toward the right. Toward the left, I could see clearly—but only if I moved my head back and forth, like windshield wipers, to view what I was trying to see. To view anything to the right of me, I had to turn my head so my left eye could do the work.

Chapter 3

I was suddenly cross-eyed, unable to see anything that was not straight in front of me.

This was pretty scary stuff.

I had never heard of an injury like this. I couldn't move my eyes up or down, left or right. I feared I had had a stroke.

The job quickly became unimportant. My sons drove me home where I rested overnight. The next day, Susan took me to a local ophthalmologist. His diagnosis? Thyroid cancer. He referred me to a prominent eye doctor at a teaching hospital in Boston.

We arranged an appointment for the same day. This doctor spewed out his impressive credentials, asked a few questions, examined me, and shared his preliminary diagnosis: stroke.

Was it cancer or was it stroke? We were bouncing between the two like ping-pong balls in a hotly contested match.

Whichever diagnosis was correct, I clearly needed an MRI.

Another MRI! First it was my shoulder ... now my eyes. Goddammit! I am not getting an MRI.

I remembered all too well the fear and how it chiseled away my ego and tough self-image. To run a business with demanding tenants and short-sighted roofers, I needed to be tough.

Even so, I knew I didn't have a choice. An MRI meant the difference between life and death. To restore my vision or, worse yet, to avoid a premature death from an undetected cancer or a dangerous stroke, I would have to climb into that *thing* again. Facing my mortality was a shock.

(I wonder now if this was an ominous foreshadowing.) No matter, we needed to find out why my eye was locked and my vision impaired.

With orders for a stat MRI, staff guided Susan and I to an elevator and pushed the down button. When it stopped, we couldn't tell how far below ground level we'd traveled. Fluorescence was the only light. No fresh air, no sunlight … no windows. Vastly different from my open-air roofing environment. I felt claustrophobia seep into my blood vessels as I walked the passageway.

A vein in my temple twitched.

I understood that the disorienting remoteness of the room had its reason: MRIs are powerful machines that vibrate and oscillate while making thunderous noises, pounding the surfaces on which they are installed. They need stable foundations low in the ground.

I disliked heights but made a good living conquering my fear. In fact I hated heights so much that when my wife and I traveled, I refused to stay above the third floor.

Of course, that aggravated Susan, who preferred more expansive views from her hotel rooms. Balcony views make me nervous and I can't enjoy myself. To be up high, I have to be "on alert" to feel safe. I can't enjoy myself without intensely monitoring the environment to make certain safety ropes and precautions are in place.

My aversion to heights notwithstanding, I found out I didn't like the bowels of the earth any better.

As we entered the dimly lit lower level of the hospital, my stomach churned, reminding me of the anxiety I felt on tar and gravel roof jobs. To create a smooth spread, we often heated the asphalt to its flashpoint of 475°. Asphalt is finicky. Outside temperatures, burner size, different kettles with different levels of coking (built up burner debris) in the tubes—so many varying elements made the process difficult to control.

We monitored smoke color constantly. A change from grey to misty-green meant an explosion was imminent. When the smoke greened, you'd have to race from the roof to climb down the ladder to the kettle where you'd kill the burners, eliminate the oxygen, and scramble for extinguishers. We had seconds to prevent the kettle from exploding into a fireball of deadly asphalt. Whenever I saw the smoke turn green, a panic impulse sent adrenaline and bolts of energy for the fast action needed to avert a disaster.

MRIs instigated the same thoughts of danger, as powerful as those from bad kettle days. As we approached the MRI room, I smelled and looked for smoke.

My antennas went up at the sharp contrast between my preferred fresh air and sunlight—against the stale hospital ventilation and sickly fluorescent lights.

My mood soured. Susan knew I was scared and admitted she was, too. She worried about my diagnosis; I worried about the MRI.

As we approached the intake area, I felt myself melting into a puddle—exactly like my MRI experience in 2003. When we neared the machine, the worry of claustrophobia gripped me by the throat. My eyes widened as I stared at the looming monstrosity.

Fear and Self-Doubt, lurking in their corners, glared back.

I envisioned their forms as fierce twin lions stalking their prey, watching and waiting to pounce. Fear and Self-Doubt owned the room. The two bullies patrolled their space like the caged, hungry lions they were.

And they watched my every move.

On edge, I answered the medical tech's mundane questions about past health conditions, family history, blah, blah, blah. Then came The Big Question: "Sir, are you claustrophobic?"

"No," I cockily asserted.

After all, it had been eleven years since my last MRI fiasco. Surely I had the growth to move beyond past insecurities, the skill to finesse my way through? The grit to ignore the slow tightening grip at my throat?

Both lions looked up. They rumbled and licked their lips.

As I climbed onto the MRI platform, I felt the lions' breath on my shoulders. While the technician locked my head into the helmet restraint, I imagined myself as a gatekeeper with both hands on a swinging gate, the lions on one side, me on the other as I grappled to keep the gate between us.

I felt the magnetic force of the MRI pull one hand from the gate. The lions pressed closer. They knew—and I knew—this weakened my ability to keep them out. Fear and Self-Doubt roared at my frailty, salivating.

The doctors relied on a series of sequenced pictures of my brain to gauge any damage or delineate any growths near my eyes. Each set of pictures takes about ten minutes. The imaging takes about an hour. I was locked to a stationary platform with a domed ceiling less than five inches from my face and knew, if I moved at all, I'd have to start the process all over again.

Sweat rolled down my cheeks. I didn't dare brush it away. My heart raced and my mind kept up with it. I was losing control.

I didn't think I was invincible, but I felt damn tough. I had built a roofing business from the ground up. I had survived my house burning down and the ensuing false arson charges. I had built a real estate company so my family and I could sustain our livelihood. Proof that *everything* could be conquered, even my fear of heights. How? I did it by working methodically, one step at a time.

Calm down. Focus on the prize, I reminded myself.

Self-Doubt pawed at my shoulder.

I squeezed the button. Mr. Smart Aleck chimed in, "Are you okay?"

"No!" My panicked shout rang across the room. "Get me out of here! NOW!"

I quickly changed back to street clothes and met Susan in the waiting area. She had never seen me fail like this. She was shaken, but not as shaken as I was.

I was demoralized.

The doctor who ordered the MRI would never receive the results.

What would we do? I couldn't tolerate the machine that would've provided the information and the path we needed.

They don't know the depths of my fear. And I wasn't capable of fully describing its depths, its hold on my sanity. Nor could I explain how I felt permanently bruised by my own weakness. How much I hated the machine and the entire undertaking forced upon me.

Because I was so distraught, we secured a prescription for Valium. Since the hospital pharmacy was already closed because of the late hour, we knew it would take fifteen minutes to get to our car and out of the parking garage. Instead, we opted to Uber to the nearest pharmacy.

It was closed.

After checking business hours online, we raced to a nearby Walgreens.

Valium in hand, I reluctantly tossed back a dose with a sip of bottled water while our Uber driver circled back to the hospital.

The technician squeezed me back into the MRI schedule.

By now I was spent ... and the lions were restless. Hungry. The Valium didn't put the lions to sleep, but I felt some of its effects.

Sweaty and anxious, I stripped down again, modesty by now nearly nonexistent. I tossed the sheets around me and slid onto the platform. The machine jolted backward, engulfing me once again. Although at this point I just wanted it over, nevertheless, I attempted an experimental squirm to see if I could get out by myself—just in case the power went out and Mr. Smart Aleck forgot about me and no one remembered I was stuck there.

I couldn't move my body at all. Not even a tiny wiggle's worth.

The lions pounced.

"Get me out! I can't do this!"

An MRI wasn't in the cards this day.

The next day, Susan made an appointment with a doctor with whom she had worked for several years at New England Sinai Hospital. Dr. Eneyni, a bright neuro-opthalmologist, had his own office an hour away.

We arrived and were ushered into his inner office. He asked me to stand directly in front of him while he held up his right hand.

"Without moving your head, follow my pointing finger only with your eyes, Steve," he said. But I couldn't follow the movement without moving my whole head.

He wrinkled his brow in thought. I sensed a flipping switch that lit his face in remembrance: he had seen my symptoms before.

Within five minutes of our arrival, he gave his preliminary diagnosis.

"I believe you have a condition called third nerve palsy, Steve." Dr. Eneyni offered a simple explanation: "I think your vision loss resulted from inflammation and perhaps dehydration from the intense heat of the rooftop. This froze the optical nerves in your eyes."

His theory was welcome news.

If I'm lucky, this condition is reversible. Please, let it be reversible.

The clincher? He needed a brain scan to rule out any other potential dangers, like aneurysm, cancer, or stroke.

After listening to my rant about MRIs, Dr. Eneyni suggested an open-bore MRI.

"Open-bore? I didn't know there were different types." The idea immediately piqued my interest.

The open-bore machine, he explained, is larger but produces slightly lesser quality images.

A larger machine? As in, I might not feel so closed in?

"Though less clear, the images just might work, Steve. They only need to be clear enough to confirm my diagnosis."

My pulse quickened.

"Open-bores have a significantly larger entry point," he explained. "I predict it won't be as traumatic for you."

Why wasn't I told sooner that there was an option like this?

Dr. Eneyni arranged for this novel scan.

Although I still didn't welcome another MRI experience, my reluctance lessened and loosened when I met with a new technician at a new facility. Friendly and comfortable with people who experienced claustrophobia, he matter-of-factly walked me into the test area.

I was relieved to see a significantly larger enclosure. This wasn't at all like the tube-shaped caskets I'd been squeezed into earlier. And my head would not be locked down! No catcher's mask this time. I was more than willing to keep myself still, deathly still.

I didn't so much as blink an eye for twenty minutes. No lions crept in.

I did it! I managed my first successful MRI!

And I survived with my courage, my bruised ego, and my slightly damaged, macho self-image intact … mostly.

The scan came back negative. No evidence of cancer. No stroke. No aneurysm.

Dr. Eneyni's diagnosis turned out to be spot-on. I did, indeed, have third nerve palsy. He prescribed rest, aspirin, and lots of water … but no direct sunlight.

Within a week the blurred vision in my right eye cleared. A week later, my left eye unlocked. You can't imagine how much joy that gave me.

At first my eye movement was barely perceptible. Then I started to catch occasional glimpses of the view to my left. It was a crazy-good, almost-orgasmic feeling.

My range of vision grew without me rocking my head like a pendulum. Gradually, my left eye could sweep left and return to center. I was no longer cross-eyed and crazy looking. I could see normally again!

What a great feeling recovery is, like a morning sunrise inside your head.

Even now, chakras shiver their way up and down my spine whenever I think about that moment. I was one lucky guy. I had dodged a bullet.

Timeline: 2016

Two years after the palsy episode, I injured my left knee while running in the winter on an icy trail. I had worn crampons, metal teeth attached to footwear to create traction on the ice. Unfortunately, they caused me to overwork and, consequently, tear a ligament.

Yup. Another MRI.

Happily, I learned that my open-bore tolerance remained. Though the lions were still present, the gate was securely shut. I managed to fight through my fear.

The surgery that followed was a success. I rehabbed my knee and returned to my passion for endurance sports.

But those menacing lions hid in their cave, just out of view, waiting patiently for their next chance, their next meal.

Lessons Learned

- Hydration is vitally important to your health and well-being.

- An open-bore MRI is a tolerable experience.

- Work isn't worth sacrificing your health.

- Diagnosing is difficult and doctors do make mistakes; second opinions are worth the effort.

Questions Begging Answers

- Can my claustrophobia be eased? Eliminated?

- Can I tame the hungry lions, Fear and Self-Doubt?

- Why do MRIs insist on an active role in my life?

Chapter 4

WHAT AM I MISSING?

We are all just a car crash, a diagnosis, an unexpected phone call, or a broken heart away from becoming a completely different person.
— SAMUEL DECKER THOMPSON

Timeline: May 21, 2018

At age sixty-three, I sensed my brain losing acuity.

I must be getting old! My shoulders shook with my silent chuckle.

But it was real. I was slipping.

Lately, small issues cropped up; missed appointments were no longer the exception. I had less patience and tolerance. Normally I'd cut slack for anyone. Even if they cut me off on the road, or were late on their rent, or acted pissy toward me. I had plenty of room for them in my wheelhouse of understanding. But, now?

Obviously, the years have caught up with me and are beginning to show.

One day at the office, I received an annoying call from a tenant about some rubbish someone had lazily dropped—*outside* the dumpster! Irritated that there was one more lazy, callous, and uncaring person in my life than I needed, I headed off to check out the situation,

On the way, I inexplicably drove my trusted, go-anywhere Toyota truck over a granite curb in the center of Stoughton, near my office. My reliable Tacoma had 128,000 miles, hundreds of plowed driveways, and thousands of jobs in its resume. I liked my old truck.

Actually, I loved my old truck. After seven or eight years, to people like me who live out of a vehicle, a truck is like a faithful old dog with personality. The stuff you cart in it practically leaps at you when you need it. When you change trucks or get in an accident, you are a mess of non-emotional losses. A trauma, nonetheless.

I lumbered out, dazed. I wasn't hurt. I would have thought someone might have honked the horn, or even stopped to offer help. No one cared, at least not enough to do anything. Thankfully, as far as I could tell, no one else was involved in the accident.

In disbelief, I walked around, surveying for damage, which was minor. Cars buzzed by on busy Route 138 as I tried to figure out what had happened. How had I gotten here? I shrugged and climbed back into the driver's seat.

I backed off the curb. I could still drive. But, where to?

Where did I live? Which way was my house? Had I hit my head? I decided to drive home, but ... which direction? Because I often biked to work, I remembered the distance was six miles. I fumbled forward, drove down dead-end roads, reaching the end and coming back.

It was dark and cloudy. I looked ahead several hundred yards. The tall green pines on either side swallowed the road and confused me further.

I decided to take a right, perhaps looking for a shortcut. I recognized the name of a daycare business that I knew wasn't on my way home. Strange.

Maybe they moved, I thought.

The gas gauge hovered near empty and I got nervous.

How long have I been driving? And where's my house?

I didn't know.

Three hours later, I found my driveway and pulled up to the garage. The sensor lights came on, and I rubbed my eyes. I stumbled toward the house. My back ached and exhaustion swept over me.

I didn't yet know it, but *She* had arrived. *She* had smashed my truck. *She* had taken away my compass and my memory!

To survive cancer, there is an element of luck. A car accident might not seem like good luck, but it was. This accident would introduce me to *you-know-who.*

She was no longer sneaking around, working and lurking menacingly in secret, while destroying my brain. *She* was outing herself and in the nick of time—a good turn of events.

To fight cancer, you must know your enemy, know who *She* is and where *She* thrives. Most of us know someone who died from cancer, who didn't discover the disease until it was too late. Fortunate ones, like me, get a chance to fight back against this mysterious miscreant who rips our lives apart.

Lessons Learned

- Health problems can appear suddenly and almost without warning.

- Don't brush aside sudden health issues in your life or blame them on the aging process.

- Seek medical input.

Questions Begging Answers

- After years of a clean driving record, why am I suddenly sloppy at the wheel?

- Why do I feel vague and lost?

- Where is my sense of direction?

Chapter 5

SHUT DOWN AT A FOGGED-IN AIRPORT

My remember-er is broken but my forget-er works perfectly.
— UNKNOWN

The day after the accident, I drove to a nearby Lowes contractor yard to pick up some loam for our garden. Or it might have been Home Depot ... I can't remember exactly.

I got lost in the store's garden department—a mere ten parallel rows inside the store, yet I couldn't find the exit. The simple layout confused me. As I paced back and forth a full hour, searching for the right aisle, fear mounted inside me. I couldn't remember whether I had visited the aisle I was in once, or a hundred times. None of the aisles were familiar.

Only a few people floated around the perimeter, and none looked friendly. I was coming undone and probably looked disheveled and frightened.

Two hours after I left the store—with the wrong loam—I returned home to a scathing rebuke from my wife. Where had I been? Why didn't I have the loam I went for? I didn't know.

Susan couldn't understand what was wrong with me. Impatiently, she had waited over three hours for me to get home, and then I arrived confused, clearly acting unlike myself.

My wife didn't yet know, but *She* knew, and I now knew I was in a dogfight with this intruder who suddenly controlled my brain.

No longer could I trust my own judgment, my own thoughts, my own mind.

As I lost memory, pieces of myself had slipped away. *She* was busy, and her plan was working. I often couldn't remember what I had done the previous day. I couldn't plan ahead anymore. I lost track of appointments and time. I lost my way driving from my home to my office. A distance of just six miles.

Changes in my mental status and vision seemed gradual, yet strikingly sudden. At the onset, I didn't notice an inability to focus. I didn't recognize the small but growing obstruction *She* scratched into my left eye, even when it grew and altered my vision like blinding fog that rolls in from the Mediterranean on cold mornings to signal a change in seasons.

When I couldn't see an object clearly, I compensated by unconsciously swiveling my head sideways to create better vision. *She* was gradually shutting down my sight day by day and took me from competent to incompetent within a short time. I had worked my whole life to learn and run my real estate and construction business with my sons, a challenging task even with solid capabilities.

She mocked my years of hard work.

Looking back now, it was obvious *She* had been chipping away for quite some time in her workshop. An incident earlier in May had hinted at what was to come.

My son Dave and I had arrived at the construction site for his new house. We were going to stake out the foundation on the land he had purchased.

He, his wife, Rory, and I had worked really hard to get a great deal on a beautiful, fourteen-acre wooded lot for their new home. We needed to locate the house and garage on the land so we knew which trees to clear.

Avid naturalists, Rory and Dave wanted to remove as few trees as possible. But, as we measured off the house from the surveyor stakes, I couldn't seem to orient myself correctly.

"Dad!" Dave yelled, "Don't you see it? This is simple. The garage will come off the house in this direction! We'll need to cut down this big pine tree."

"Dave!" I yelled back, "The garage is on this side."

"No, Dad," he pointed emphatically at the plans, "it's on the other side. It goes this way."

Pre-cancer, this would have been obvious to me. A non-issue.

Of course, at that time, I hadn't yet realized *She* was staking out territory in my head. Neither had Dave.

During the following weeks, I continued at my jobs, but in hindsight, I started to shy away from detail and computer work. My part of our family business included a significant amount of writing and documentation for billing, filing permits, and coordinating contractors and customer requests. I couldn't focus.

And then my weird disorientation in Lowe's and my inability to orient at Dave's place happened.

What the heck is going on with me?

Chapter 5

Before long, I couldn't walk from one end of our 2200-square-foot office to the bathroom and know how to get back. *She* scraped away at my memory thread by thread. Memory reminds us who we are, but *She* didn't want me to know.

I hadn't seen any of this coming. Cancer was a tornado unexpectedly spinning toward me on the horizon. I couldn't control it, couldn't slow it, couldn't stop it. I had been busy running my own business—and minding my business—for sixty-three years. There was plenty to do as husband, father, grandfather, friend, professor, and business owner.

I don't remember much of that time. It remains hazy. With my brain on overload, my lights steadily dimmed.

Lessons Learned

- Like a lost child, I was disoriented and defenseless. *She* is powerful enough to bring you to your knees in humility.

- Swallow your pride.

- Rely on family to pick up the slack.

Questions Begging Answers

- How much more memory will I lose?

- What else will happen to me?

- Now that my family knows, can we work our way out of this hole together?

Chapter 6

BROKEN BRAIN, LOTS OF PAIN

I was in a maze.
No matter which way I turned,
it was the wrong way.
— Umberto Eco

Timeline: June 1, 2018

I awoke disoriented.

What day is it? Is it still May?

I couldn't even remember the year. Was it 2018? I didn't know. My equilibrium was off. I clumsily tripped over my slippers. I wasn't drunk, but it felt that way. I couldn't walk or think straight.

As is my routine, I looked outside and tried to determine the exact time I woke up, an odd little guessing game, my morning ritual. Some days I'm off by an hour or more, but most of the time I'm within minutes.

I figured the time was 5:35 a.m. I looked but couldn't read the time on my Apple watch, even with its large digits.

Guess I need a bigger screen now. Getting older sucks.

I chuckled at my vanity, squinted my eyes, and tried to refocus. I could see the watch face but simply couldn't figure out what the numbers on the dial meant.

That's strange.

I looked again and again. I realized I actually could see the numbers but they didn't register. Didn't compute. No matter how long I stared at them, I couldn't decipher the time.

What day is it again? Geez, I didn't know.

I tried harder to remember. I recalled white flowers in the driveway. May flowers?

Maybe it's the last week of May?

I didn't know for sure.

"Siri, what day is it?" I demanded. She didn't respond. I had forgotten we disconnected her.

I forced myself to think.

Am I dreaming? What is going on?

Focusing on anything, even a mere detail, was suddenly difficult. Strange as it sounds, thinking confused me more than just resting and ignoring things. But I clawed at myself to figure out what was happening.

I walked in circles around our twelve-foot kitchen island, looking for ... something. But ... what?

Susan came into the kitchen. I hadn't noticed her watching me circle the island for five minutes because I was that focused ... or lost in thought. Or lost.

"What are your plans today?" Her tone was hesitant, uncertain.

"I don't know," I mumbled. I didn't even know why I was in the kitchen.

With more insistence she repeated, "What are you doing today?"

I didn't like her pressuring me. "I don't know!" I was agitated. Edgy.

Susan put her hand on my forearm and led me to a kitchen chair. "Honey, I'm calling Dr. Weinreb. You need to see him."

Dr. Weinreb is my primary care physician (PCP), our incredible family doctor, and a personal friend. I like him and usually don't mind seeing him even though I hate doctor visits, especially annual check-ups and the embarrassing tests that come with them.

"I don't need a doctor. I'll be fine." I saw no need to waste time when I should be on the job.

"I'm worried. You know, Steve," she reminded me, "you struggled to find your way home from the eye doctor yesterday. And now ... this."

It was true. The day before, I had been confused and couldn't find the roads I usually took. My phone was dead so I couldn't call. I kept driving and finally found my way home.

I guess maybe something really is happening. And it doesn't sound good.

After she described my confusion, Dr. Weinreb insisted we go straight to the emergency room.

I called my sons to check on our work for the day only to learn Susan had already alerted them that I wouldn't be there. Everyone insisted I go directly to the hospital. I objected half-heartedly, but deep down I struggled with the thought that my brain was completely compromised.

I finally agreed to go to the emergency department at South Shore Hospital in Weymouth, Massachusetts, a thirty-minute drive from home.

It dawned on me that I knew how a fish feels when it realizes it has swallowed bait and is now on a hook—a terrible, sinking feeling. I couldn't free myself from these disorienting perceptions and thoughts. I couldn't get off the hook.

Susan insisted on driving; I begrudgingly got into the passenger seat. The intake process at the hospital was normal, but not for me. I was in a fog. I was asked the typical questions about insurance, age, history, allergies ... but, for the life of me, I couldn't come up with the answers.

After a thirty-minute wait, we saw a freshly minted young doctor who accomplished the admission intake and set up a CT scan. CTs use radiation (not magnetic pulses), which carries its own dangers. I accepted the risk.

I wore regular street clothes, a small comfort that I didn't have to undress and don the bed sheet medical people think passes for clothing. Far less noisy than an MRI, this machine didn't necessitate a head restraint so the scan was tolerable. I made it through. The lions were in hiding.

After a short wait to read the images, our young doctor met us in a private room. He stammered nervously as he addressed us. "Mr. Kelley, you—you have a mass in your head."

Susan paled. With my loss of memory and some recent peculiar actions on my part, she suspected the news. It was still tough to hear. In her intense eighteen years of patient care as a physician assistant, she had become familiar with terminal disease. She imagined the worst.

I didn't understand the severity of his message. "What's a mass?"

Before he could answer, I made a bad joke about not going to church and paying for it now. I felt sorry for the young doctor.

His answers were filled with could-bes: It could be a tumor. It could be benign. It could be something else.

He didn't know why I was losing my vision. Strangely the situation made him more uncomfortable than I felt. From his reaction, I guessed this was the first time he had to give a patient bad news.

"You need more testing and you need it *now*."

The urgency in his voice penetrated my fog, but I needed a break. I asked the doctor if we could wait outside. I wanted, I *needed* to tell my family what was going on.

Standing outside suddenly faced with exactly which person to call first, I got stuck mentally. I didn't want anyone in my family to feel slighted or to hear the news secondhand. I tried to figure out how to place a conference call to include them all.

I wasn't great at technology even before the mass that crowded my head, but now with impaired vision and a confused state of mind, I was worse. Jittery with her own fears, Susan wasn't any more competent in the moment.

An idea hit me. I called my best friend, Luis, who had a strong technical background, and explained my predicament.

As soon as he got over his shock at my situation, he quickly rose to the occasion. "I'll do anything to help, *mi amigo*. Tell me the phone numbers you want conferenced."

Five minutes later Luis called back. "Steve, everyone is on the phone except Susan's son Dave."

"Wait!" Susan chimed in. "I'll call him on my phone."

As soon as she reached Dave, we huddled together and started the conversation with both phones on speaker.

"Hi, guys. We have some news. I just had a CT scan at South Shore Hospital. I have some kind of a mass in my head. They're taking me to Brigham for more testing."

"What's going on, Dad?" Dave asked.

"We don't know yet. I just wanted to give you all a heads up. I'm going to be okay." I had a hesitant but intentional laugh. "At least, I think."

With no little urgency, our doctor was busy himself, arranging to have me admitted at Brigham and Women's Hospital in Boston where a brain MRI was readily available and would be read instantly.

This is serious. The thought pounded at my head, demanding acceptance.

By now, the mere mention of those combined three letters, M—R—I, raised my blood pressure. But I didn't have time to fret. The ambulance arrived, its white, blue, and red strobe lights flashing annoyingly. A mass of commotion engulfed me as orders were issued, attendants darted, equipment clanked.

"Guys," I yelled into the phone, trying to override the noise, "the ambulance is here. We're on our way." I plugged one ear with my finger. "I'll call you when we know more. Don't worry. I'm going to be fine."

I was startled to suddenly find myself loaded—and restrained—on a gurney.

I preferred to walk under my own power; the attendants insisted I follow protocol.

A confused nurse at Brigham and Women's ER insisted we follow *her* protocol: a standard intake, which would cost us another precious thirty minutes. Susan wouldn't have it. Upset and frightened, she laid into the nurse.

"This is supposed to be a direct admit!" An experienced hospital professional herself, Susan knew the lingo and the process. This poorly informed nurse wasn't going to B.S. *her*. "Get my husband to the MRI area STAT!"

Susan handily dispensed with the gatekeeper.

As we arrived at the imaging area, I suddenly roused from my stupor: I was going to have another MRI.

One minute I was at home, confused by odd vision issues, and the next I was being asked to disrobe. To climb into the perilous lions' den yet again.

Like a lawnmower starting up, I jolted noisily into motion. "I'm *not* doing an MRI," I told them. "I won't!"

Everyone responded at once in a flurry of disconcertion, confusion, exasperation. And noisy disruption.

My heart pounded. I paced back and forth in the hallway, trying to settle my nerves. Susan and the medical team hovered impatiently. Dr. Lakshmi Nayak and the oncology lymphoma team at Brigham and Women's would need the MRI imaging.

Dr. Tim Smith, the team's neurosurgeon, required the scan in order to biopsy the mass. There was no other way to determine the type of tumor that had taken up residency in my brain. Saving my life—yes, we were literally at that critical point—depended on what they saw in the scan. My treatment plan would be designed on what they discovered about the tumor.

I knew they were disgusted with my refusal to cooperate. I also knew I didn't care.

My head hurts. I wonder if it's the tumor.

I was surrounded by brilliant people all telling me what to do. I wanted to shout them down and run away, but I couldn't.

"Just do it, Steve," Susan implored. "Just do what they're telling you. You can do it, if you try."

I feel stupid. I can't think straight. I can't do this.

"No!" I repeated. "No!"

Totally beside herself, Susan tried to convince me to go back into the monster. *Everyone* told me I had no choice—one massive, confusing mess of voices ordering me into the MRI.

"I won't. I'll die first. I can't do it."

So we argued. I felt pressure at my shoulders. The same pressure as when I was being shoved backwards on that rumbling machine. The lions were there, and I wasn't even in the room.

Sweat rolled down my forehead. My throat constricted. Claustrophobia made me irrational. I was terrified. Terrified—not of dying, terrified of the machine.

After consulting among themselves, they admitted me to the

hospital. The next day a surgical resident anesthesiologist, Dr. Ross, consulted with us. He was sincere and tried hard to come up with a solution.

"If this were your father," Susan asked, "what would you do? We can't just let him sit here."

My wife had framed it perfectly. Dr. Ross nodded in understanding. "Let's find a way to get this MRI done."

The two of them conceived a new plan. Would I accept sedation?

"What about IV Ativan?" Susan suggested.

"That works for some people," Dr. Ross responded. "It has to be well-controlled with a staff nurse by his side because it's a more complicated process with greater risks."

Susan gripped my forearm with urgency. "Will you try the IV Ativan, Steve?"

Too tired and beaten down to put up a fight, I murmured my response. "Yeah, okay."

I was tired of everyone pushing me to do the MRI, but the mass in my head had taken its toll. Even *I* knew I had to do something.

Imaging for a brain tumor is a two-step process. First, the machine scans for density and skeletal form. Next, a contrast dye is injected intravenously into the blood to allow the MRI to graph abnormalities. Using two sets of images—pre- and post-contrast dye—the medical team identifies the tumor's specific location and size.

My guide-at-the-side nurse explained the procedure as she inserted IV lines into my arm. A specific dosage of IV Ativan had been ordered based on my weight. She gauged my response. I was tense but confident in her calm manner, experience, and efficiency.

She injected me with the IV Ativan just before the platform rolled me into the tube, assuring me she would be in the room the whole time. Fortunately, the IV Ativan began its slow rolling knockout.

I shut my eyes for a moment. As did the lions.

"You're done, Mr. Kelley." Her words roused me from my nap.

Groggy, I needed assistance from the bed and into a wheelchair—where I fell asleep again.

I awoke in a hospital room, surrounded by family.

The "wet read" arrived—the preliminary analysis provided by MRI specialists to attending doctors. The verdict? A tumor the size of a pimple-popping fat avocado.

An avocado?

It can't be that big. No way. Exactly what kind of cancer is this, anyway? And, what does all this mean?

Results in hand, Dr. Smith scheduled a biopsy to make the final determination. Blood and tissue samples would determine our next steps.

Lessons Learned

- I'm not as tough as I thought I was; it doesn't matter.

- To survive, find ways to get through and fight another day.

- MRIs are necessary. Figure it out. Get it done!

Questions Begging Answers

- How do we fight what we don't know?

- What answers will my biopsy provide?

- How will this affect my family?

Chapter 1

IT'S NOT BRAIN SURGERY. OOPS, YES, IT IS!

My wife had been trepanned already,
and she spoke very highly of it.
— LORD JAMES NEIDPATH

Trepanning is the thousands-year-old practice of drilling holes in the skull to cure various ailments. I don't recommend it.

Astonishingly, I found myself hospitalized at Dana-Farber Cancer Institute for a mass in my brain. Dr. Tim Smith, the neurosurgeon in whose hands I must put my trust and my brain, intended to trepan my skull by performing a biopsy. He would drill a hole to remove tissue for diagnostic purposes.

I need this biopsy like I need a hole in my head, I thought.

I was wrong. In fairness to Dr. Smith, I actually *did* need that hole in my head.

He entered the room in a hurried, no-nonsense fashion. At six feet or taller, he was trim and athletic-looking in his blue scrubs and appeared to have come directly from surgery.

His urgent mission was to assess me to better prep himself for the upcoming surgery.

In casual conversations with buddies, we had an expression for those who made hard work out of easy jobs or who made ridiculous mistakes under simple conditions.

"Well, he's no brain surgeon," we'd say before roaring at our cleverness.

But Dr. Smith *was* a brain surgeon. A talented, skilled brain surgeon highly regarded by his peers and colleagues. Or so we'd been told.

Will he pass muster with me?

My earlier hospitalization had steered us to Dana-Farber. Susan and I hadn't had the leisure to shop hospitals and institutions, to vet surgeons, to sift through resumes and recommendations. Sure, this place had a great reputation, but the whole situation had spiraled out of control. My control.

It's not something planned or chosen, like an elective surgery. I didn't ask for any of this! I just landed here. Someone or other thought it was the right place.

But is it?

"How are you feeling, Steve?" Dr. Smith's rather pedestrian question was, obviously, the start of his assessment.

I didn't think he really needed to know. Instead, I sensed he asked strictly to hear how I would answer, how I would frame my response. Whether I was a gamer. It was all part of his assessment.

Bring on the questions!

"Steve, I hear you don't like MRIs," he commented, eyeing me closely.

I figured he didn't expect an answer. He simply presented the possibility to reassure me that he had the information necessary for the biopsy.

Two can play this game.

I narrowed my gaze on him. "So, what's it like, Dr. Smith? The prestige of being a neurosurgeon? The fame?" I tossed questions right back at him, turning the tables.

Now *I* was the inquisitor.

I was mildly shocked at his sudden modesty. He wanted no part of that conversation. No fame; he preferred anonymity, anonymity to the point that he warned me not to email him. He didn't answer emails, either.

I like this guy, I decided, a bit shocked at the discovery. *And he's obviously smart, super intelligent.*

No wonder Dana-Farber was held in high regard.

Making an abrupt assessment of my own, I placed myself in his capable hands.

"Drill away!"

Lessons Learned

- Don't try to undermine your doctor or underplay your situation.

- Respect your specialists. They know what they are doing.

Questions Begging Answers

- What is my final, definitive diagnosis?

- What will this mean to Susan and me? To our marriage? Our family?

Chapter 8

TIME IS BRAIN!

*Unhappiness is the permanent bruise each and every
one of us gets when we come face to face with reality.*
—José Ortega y Gasset

Timeline: June 6, 2018

Adversity has power.

You wrestle away that power by conquering the challenges adversity brings.

The first step to beat my challenge—cancer—was to identify the adversary, to know who and where *She* was. Something or someone does you the huge favor of letting you know. The earlier the better. Finding out hurts. In a split-second, you go from invincible—somehow we all think we are—to aware of the potential immediacy of your demise.

Your notice is sent faster than a FedEx overnight on steroids. Envision that package with a red devil stamp on it. Open it, and you see your E-Z Life Pass has been pitchfork punched.

The Grim Reaper stomped his boot prints all over what was once a pristine ticket. Despite the obvious (we all die), it is a tremendous shock when death first whispers in your ear, "I'm coming for *you*."

My news arrived after Dr. Smith's competent biopsy.

I lay in a hospital bed on the eighth floor of Brigham and Women's Hospital in Boston—in the stark, clinically clean white room anchored by a single chair. Director of the institute's CNS Lymphoma Center, Dr. Lakshmi Nayak held center stage. I had trouble focusing.

Both Dr. Nayak and the physician assistant, Aleks, who accompanied her, were young and attractive. For some reason, I had expected a reliable, older, *male* doctor—a bias about to be turned on its head.

From the corner of my eye, I could see that Susan was equally surprised. I had the feeling that if I focused too long on them, my wife would elbow me in the ribs. Obviously, she thought about it but didn't. Afterward, we agreed they made it hard for me to concentrate.

And that was just an early manifestation of my issues.

We had yet to witness how, as *She* progressed, my brain would spiral into what felt like a drunken stupor. I wouldn't be able to focus. To concentrate. I would be even more disoriented, like being high without a drug, as if someone scissor-cut all the connections in my brain. Someone did. *She* cut those connections. Before long, I wouldn't be able to find the bathroom in my own house. From my own bed. Only eight feet away. That was a joke *She* must have loved to see play out.

She certainly wasn't well intentioned. Maybe *She* had a rough upbringing. Perhaps *She* felt cursed and wanted to share her misery.

But in this moment, it was Dr. Nayak and Aleks's job to deliver the diagnosis we dreaded to hear: the biopsy showed I had a rare brain disease called primary central nervous system lymphoma. CNS lymphoma is rare—only three in 1,000,000—and survival rates are dismal.

Here I was, one of The Rare Three. Lucky, lucky me.

As a specialist in CNS lymphoma, Dr. Nayak knew the drill. She spoke straightforwardly about the harsh reality of the disease—while balancing the message with deliberately soft-spoken advice about hopeful treatments.

We breathed in the severity of the message slowly.

Dr. Nayak carefully toed a neutral line about the treatment. Until she broached the subject of MRIs. When she suggested addition scans would be needed, I balked.

"Nope. No way."

I hated those machines. Each time I had been in an MRI, they stripped me of my confidence. I didn't feel kindly toward the technicians who operated them, either, even though I recognized my attitude was a much-too-broad stroke to paint all MRI professionals. I didn't yet know I would find many empathetic souls to help me through.

Empathy is difficult to maintain as a medical professional when everyone they see is in pain. It's hard to honor that pain. It's even harder to take that pain home and stay balanced, so they learn to build a shell, to close off. It's necessary. I know, because I live with it: my wife is a physician assistant.

I shook my head, adamant. "I won't go in that machine again. I'd rather die."

Susan, with her medical background and pragmatism, allied with Dr. Nayak. "Steve, listen to what they are telling you."

"*Time*—is—brain, Steve!" Dr. Nayak asserted sternly, with emphasis on time. "You can't wait. We'll need many more images of your brain in the months ahead."

"What do you mean?" I was perplexed. "How long do I have if we don't treat it?"

She squinted her eyes. "If our treatments don't work, you probably have three to six weeks."

Alarmed, Susan grabbed my arm.

Almost before the revelation could sink in, Dr. Nayak continued. "We specialize in your disease, in CNS lymphoma. Granted, there are no guarantees, but our treatments are very effective."

Unlike the medical professionals in the room with me, never before had I dealt with a life-threatening illness. And this was *me* they were talking about, not some vague patient. For me, this was a shocking existential threat. Something suddenly clicked in my head.

Fuck YOU, *cancer. You aren't taking me out!*

As Dr. Nayak leaned forward in her chair, she lowered her voice, even more emphatic. "Listen, Steve, your tumor is deadly and it's growing fast. Every day we don't treat you, you lose a piece of your brain."

She's talking about life or death. My life. My death, I realized with a jolt of deep understanding. *And she's telling me what I need to do to beat this bastard of a disease.*

I leaned in closer, ready to learn how to win this unexpected battle.

Lessons Learned

- No matter its severity, the sooner you find out you have cancer, the luckier you are. Early diagnosis paves the way for treatment options.

- Their duties are unreasonably difficult to perform, so use grace in your dealings with medical professionals.

- Medical professionals have to build a shell to protect themselves from too much personal pain that would otherwise prevent clear thinking, much like police officers must do.

Questions Begging Answers

- Can CNS lymphoma be reversed?

- Will it get worse?

- Can I grit my teeth through another MRI? How many more?

- Should I accept my fate with resignation?

Chapter 9

CHEMOTHERAPY TO THE RESCUE

Three things cannot be long hidden: the sun, the moon, and the truth.
— Buddhist Proverb

Timeline: June 7, 2018

Now that we knew the enemy—size, location (the occipital region, the part of the brain that controls vision and balance), and potential—we were ready to lay siege. Fortunately for me, Dr. Nayak and her team had a plan.

To further expose *Her* hiding places, more MRIs—lots of them—would be needed. It was part of the fight. I would have to do them. Definitely not something I wanted to hear, but I knew they offered the weapons necessary for this battle of a lifetime.

My lifetime.

As it turned out, *She* had built her headquarters in the blood-brain barrier sac.

Her control center, my tumor!

Again, fortunately for me, scientists and researchers and doctors galore had labored for years to develop chemical weapons for the explicit purpose of reaching, slowing, and eradicating *Her*.

Methotrexate and rituximab were the snipers for our team, designed to permeate the blood-brain barrier. With reconnaissance completed, they would travel in my blood to destroy the cancer.

CHEMOTHERAPY TO THE RESCUE

On the first day of treatment, we arrived at the hospital. No easy feat. Traffic into Boston is always painfully slow and difficult to navigate. The only parking available to us was in an underground garage, a dizzying descent into tight-quartered concrete tombs for automobiles. Susan walked fast, ever in a hurry, always worried we'd be late. I trailed behind, unable to create landmarks or know which way to go. It wasn't that I couldn't keep up. I just couldn't understand the maze in front of us, so I blindly followed my wife.

She led the way to an elevator. To a floor. To a walkway. From there, we traversed a stairwell, another walkway, and a bridge. It was a complicated pattern I couldn't decipher, couldn't understand and certainly would never remember, but our half-mile walk finally landed us in a reception area.

After checking in, we waited for a nurse to call my name.

"Steven?" She led us to a small clinical room for blood work.

There were about ten of these cubicles just off the waiting room, which held as many as fifty patients, each one typically accompanied by a family member who loyally accompanied their mate-father-sister-grandparent on these ritual pilgrimages.

Cancer's reach is wide.

We'd often encounter patients from other states, along with people from India, Africa, Europe, and China. With just a little observation, languages and clothing gave people's origin away.

The nurse offered me a seat in a two-armed chair with a small, folding edge table on each side.

"Which arm would you like me to use?"

Chapter 9

The question puzzled me. I hadn't yet realized that the "chosen" arm would become the "dependent" arm for the next eight hours.

A little shiver of premonition trickled down my spine.

The nurse sat beside me and massaged my forearm, searching for a sweet spot, the ideal vein where she would prick and slide the needle with its small yellow or red plastic couplings.

I wondered about these vampire ladies and how difficult it must be to do their job. A lot of people hate needles. They squirm in their seats, dreading the pain of the puncture.

I tried to make it easy for my nurse by falling back on my zany sense of humor, something experience had proved gets results.

"I *love* needles," I teased.

When a doubtful frown wrinkled her brow, I reassured her. "Really, I do."

She shrugged.

I responded with a shrug of my own. *Win some, lose some.*

The needle entered smoothly under my skin. She did a good job. I didn't know it then, but there would be hundreds more of these little blood-sucking episodes in my future. I didn't yet understand that upstairs in a curtain-private room on the tenth floor, I would encounter plastic lines dangling from bags of chemicals—hence the word chemotherapy. Methotrexate and rituximab would dogpaddle down the tubes and exit through the needle piercing my vein ... to swim into my blood stream.

These sniper chemicals would bridge the blood-brain barrier to seek out the cancer, maim *Her*—all in the valiant effort to protect me from *Her* vicious vise.

We had a long road ahead to travel and, hopefully, survive.

Cancer, we knew, would seriously disrupt our lives. Up to this point, we had been rather close-mouthed about my condition with some friends and colleagues. Now, hugely impending changes in routine meant that others needed to know what was happening.

Whom should I tell? And how much should I tell them?

Too much of our lives centers on money. First and foremost, I needed to confide in my banker.

Lessons Learned

- Cancer doesn't discriminate. *She* is no respecter of personages. *She* is not racist.

- Empowerment often comes from discovering others in your situation. You are not alone.

- Other medical experiences (in my case, MRIs) can be a practice, a rehearsal for what is to come.

Questions Begging Answers

- How will chemotherapy affect me?

- Can I still compete in my business?

- How much will I have to lean on my sons and wife?

Chapter 10

SPREADING
THE NEWS

Easy choices, hard life.
Hard choices, easy life.
—JERZY GREGOREK,
OLYMPIC POWERLIFTER

Timeline: June 18, 2018

Ken Ryvicker had been my banker at Rockland Trust Bank for more than twenty-five years. Small real estate companies like ours always need capital, so we depend on bankers like Ken. He is a "rainmaker" and gets things done.

As vice president for commercial loans, he was friend, confidant, and advisor. He consistently steered me into great deals. Our loans and investments aren't run-of-the-mill money-making transactions. Ken calls his special kind of business practice Relationship Banking. We feel like family because Ken treats us like family. He knows my kids, knows my wife, knows my hobbies. He is an amazing friend.

Prior to my cancer, Ken and Rockland Trust agreed to loan our thriving company $270,000 for our next group of projects. They did not loan that money to a business with an ailing CEO with, perhaps, a death sentence hanging over his head.

Even though the deal had been inked in the form of lines of credit, the bank hadn't advanced the funds for the pending deals. Ken, I decided, needed to know *before* we accessed the funds that I had brain cancer, and that neither the doctors nor I knew the outcome. I didn't want to tell Ken because it might jeopardize the transactions, but it was the right thing to do.

I didn't know whether I would survive cancer. I had no idea what my mental capacity or physical abilities were going to be after my treatment. I did know that brain cancer often has tragic results.

Would I even live to pay back the money?

My prognosis wasn't good then ... nor is it now. Without the funds, my company projects couldn't be done. It was a serious phone call, a tough one to make. It wasn't our intention, but we certainly put Ken's Relationship Banking to the test.

After the usual pleasantries, I took a deep breath. "Ken, I've got some bad news that might affect our loans. I've just had an MRI that showed a mass in my head, a tumor known as CNS lymphoma.

"I have brain cancer," I babbled on, "and I'm being treated at Dana-Farber Cancer Institute. Looks like I'll be in the hospital for an undetermined amount of time."

Unequivocally, without hesitation, Ken said, "The deal is done, Steve. The money is in the bank. Your business is solid."

But I barely heard him. "Ken, it will be three to six weeks if things don't go well. I understand if the bank needs to reassess and cancel the loan."

"No problem, Steve," he reassured me. "You've got great kids to carry on in your absence. Worry about your recovery. Your boys and I will take care of the loan."

I couldn't believe it.

"Thank you, Ken. Really, thank you." I put the phone down and cried. I swiveled around and around in my office chair, tears on my cheeks as I pondered his kind, generous response. If the shoe were on the other foot, I wasn't sure I would have given the loan with the new facts presented.

As I prepared to battle this deadly cancer, my family, my work, my entire life was disrupted. The possibility of death hung heavy. My brain function was in question. The outcome was unknown. There were no promises.

Even if treatments arrested the development of the cancer, would my brain function as before? Or would I somehow be diminished? Would I become a shadow of myself? A ... a ... vegetable?

This was the biggest challenge my family and I had ever faced. Questions and concerns were endless.

What happens if the treatment doesn't work?

Will my sons be able to run our businesses without me?

Will our medical insurance pay for all the treatments?

What about life insurance?

Will Susan be okay?

Susan! I had some life insurance, but now we needed to dig into the details. Life insurance had always been like a wart you had to look at on your hand but didn't want to pay attention to. Had I done a good enough job with coverage?

Suddenly, all those mostly ignored, warning-filled sales pitches from overly sharp insurance salespeople came home to roost.

Even though I was in my early sixties, I had not recognized any particular vulnerability. My insurance wasn't what it should have been to face this serious scenario. I was still finding other places to spend my money. Real estate investments were more important; long-term illness and funerals were something that happened to other people.

I had convinced myself I wasn't a candidate for ill health. I would live healthy and forever.

Except now I wouldn't.

Frenzied, I realized I'd made a mistake with long-reaching arms: I didn't have enough coverage to protect my family. My loose-bandaid approach exposed a giant wound in my family's financial health.

With my brain in a compromised state, I reviewed estate documents and insurance policies with my sons. We hired an estate attorney and spent days in meetings revising the trust I had set up several years earlier.

The complexities of tax law were hard to understand before my tumor. With a tumor and its associated confusion, I could barely follow the contrived logic of our obscure tax system. Fortunately, Dave took the lead.

My family and I worked frantically to understand my health issues. We wrestled with treatments and the implications of the prognosis. It became obvious that our network of friends, family, and business associates needed explanations for my absence from regular business activities along with social gatherings, birthday parties, graduations, and celebrations.

"Where's Steve?" they asked.

Rumors flew.

My business theory had always been MBWA—Management By Walking Around. In fact, our company motto is: *Don't expect what you don't inspect.* By design, I was visible daily to staff, customers, and vendors.

With cancer crossing my doorstep, tenants, customers, and vendors began noticing I wasn't around. They recognized the difference in how my sons and I now conducted ourselves and our business. We couldn't hide that the top member of the organization was gravely ill.

We knew we had to share enough information to quell the rumors.

How much should we share?

Who should get the details, and how should we disseminate them?

What do you tell friends, family, employees, and business partners like Ken?

Those were tough questions because cancer affects all of your relationships dramatically.

I use "dramatically" with cautious awareness and reluctance. Not everyone would prove to be like Ken Ryvicker. Many don't know how to respond to bad news like cancer or the death of a friend or loved one.

In the case of our business, confidence in delivery of our services is critical. Businesses fail regularly when the public loses confidence in them. I feared customers and vendors might lose faith in our construction and real estate companies if they knew I had brain cancer. All of our combined KC companies—Solid Roofing Co. Inc., KC Management, and our individual real estate LLCs—were, unexpectedly, at risk.

My fear was real, with good reason.

Everyone around me was upset while trying not to be. Nobody wanted to say too much. The science for this cancer is elusive. Even my doctors couldn't forecast with certainty a path to wellness—or whether such a path existed. They had to consider protocols, liability, and understandable concerns about how information affected Susan and me. They were necessarily tight-lipped.

With my mental status in jeopardy, uncertainty reigned. These worries gnawed at my confidence, too.

Could I make good judgments about risks, safety decisions, and construction cost estimates—the defining point of profitability? Would forty years of building my businesses go to waste? Would my companies tumble like a house of cards without me there to manage them?

I had trouble thinking and focusing on anything. I worried whether I would be able to contribute after cancer.

Am I done? Kaput? Career over, life over?

I knew honest, open communication was effective. Could I be completely transparent with everyone like I had with Ken? This was a lot to expect people to handle.

I didn't feel that I could follow my lifelong business practice of transparency.

I knew I had to communicate. Good communication is the mainstay of business. To be successful, the left hand has to know what the right hand is doing. I wanted people in my life to be as comfortable as possible with my cancer and my treatment. I also instinctively knew that humor would make it easier to share information. But little that was happening to me seemed funny at all.

I can't overstate how confused brain cancer made me. My eyesight was failing. My thought processes were interrupted. I couldn't read blueprints or simple instructions. I couldn't help my grandson put his Legos together. I had trouble replacing batteries in a flashlight; I had to study each cell to figure out how it fit. My confusion was real. It was as if someone or something hid traps in every process.

That *something* was cancer. *She* was the trapster behind everything I attempted.

So, I held back. What was happening to me ... effects of the tumor on my brain ... I didn't even confide in my family. It was scary, too scary. I didn't tell them I couldn't remember where my keys were (in my pocket), having placed them there seconds before. I couldn't admit how, midway through flossing, I couldn't remember which side of my teeth I had finished. What would they think?

Although I still drove, I didn't know how to get home from my office any more. I just felt my way home, recognizing things along the way. I could no longer describe how I made it from point A to point B. (Even now, I still struggle with directions.)

When I was first diagnosed, it seemed there was no good news to share. There was no accurate or reliable information to share. My doctors didn't know the trajectory of the disease.

Gradually as my family and our medical team knew more, I would be able to understand, open up, and share more information.

But how much?

It's a very personal decision. My wife and I did not agree; nothing new there. Susan chose the opposite direction. She chose to not share my condition with any of her coworkers, not even my initial diagnosis, the fact I had CNS lymphoma. Susan felt her performance and job situation would be adversely affected by sharing this news. I respected her opinion and her choice.

Which way was right? Susan's way worked for her; my way worked for me.

Deciding whom you tell, when you tell them, and what you tell them are some of the hazards you'll need to negotiate in your own journey.

I categorized people's responses in many different ways: The Shrinkers, who withdraw from contact, not knowing how to respond. The Shiners—like my dear friends Luis, Steven, and Ken. The Grinders—mostly family, Dave and Rory, Dave and Michelle, Phil and Jess—who stressed out but fought through (like my son Dave), who stood tall and fought (like my wife Susan), who hung on tightly no matter what (like my two friends Karen V. and Karen B.).

Most people, when they learned about my sudden health issues, seemed determined to help whenever they could.

Only a few opted out and couldn't talk to me after my diagnosis. They didn't know what to say. I think they withdrew because witnessing and dealing with a close friend's illness caused them to look at their own mortality. It is a tough thing to do, like writing your own obituary. I know; I actually wrote my obituary after I found out my diagnosis. It scared me, but not as much as MRIs do.

Others turtled in their shells, not knowing what to do. It's hard for those people, too. One friend later told me he got a sick feeling when he thought about my situation. He just couldn't bring himself to contact me.

Who am I to judge?

I shrugged it off, but I shouldn't gloss over the arrogant tendency we all have to judge others. I hadn't attended his father's funeral; I simply didn't make time in my schedule. My reasons amounted to excuses in other people's minds. How I spend my time should be my choice, and the same courtesy needs to be applied to others. It's their choice.

I accept that. Accept, too, that not everyone is a fan. Get over it. Make the best of it. Move on. Don't rehash old stuff you can't change. Use your energy to do some good in the world.

She alters lives, yours and others'. Everyone in your circle is affected differently. Sharing cancer news creates unforeseen and unpredictable consequences.

Your personal and private medical information reshapes your relationships, your job, your image, and your effectiveness.

In short, everything changes when *She* catapults into your life.

Lessons Learned

- A cancer diagnosis is equally hard on family and friends; it's a cancer roller coaster ride no one wants to take.

- Some will climb on with you, others will opt out entirely.

- Listen to your heart to know what and how much to share.

- Try not to define others by *your* cancer. Like walking into a room where a baby is sleeping, keep your footsteps soft.

- It's normal—but too easy—to become self-centered. Continue caring about and for others.

Questions Begging Answers

- How can I preserve the sanctity and separation of others' lives?

- How can I work through all my deficits?

- Will I return to my companies?

- Will I be the same man?

Chapter 11

GUTTER BALLS RULE

*Dealing with brain cancer is like
trying to bowl blindfolded.*
— STEVE KELLEY

Timeline: June 27, 2018

My family thought I'd reached a new low in dumb ideas: I insisted we all go bowling to celebrate my brain tumor. Well, actually it was my recovery that I thought we should celebrate. Pick a word—brash, presumptuous, tenuous, foolish, ridiculous—they all fit.

It was way too early to celebrate. It had only been eleven days since the diagnosis. I knew next to nothing about brain tumors or cancer. Treatment had barely started. I could no longer drive back and forth to work. How dumb this idea must have sounded to them.

I couldn't possibly have known that I would recover. My tumor made thinking and processing difficult. As I struggled to concentrate, bowling pins ricocheted off the walls of my brain. So … why not go bowling?

When I floated the idea to my wife, she quickly asserted, "Because it's not a good idea, that's why."

"You couldn't be more wrong," I brazenly fired back.

Susan gave me The Look. Surely you know The Look: a certain tilt of the head and raised eyebrow paired with a disdainful frown. She quickly reminded me of the time I uttered the same revisionist phrase when we first met. It almost cost me a second date. I rued the day my mouth moved ahead of my brain.

For the record, bowling was definitely better than her idea—and I don't even remember what her idea was. I was convinced bowling was a fantastic idea.

Although still reeling from the shock of cancer, I was determined *She* wouldn't get me down. Not even for a week. There was a reason behind my madness.

Positive focus was ingrained into my personality. For the past two decades, I had written my yearly goals:

Be happy and positive.

Be self-reliant.

Be gentle.

Use humor.

Be mature.

Make the best of every situation.

Use anabolic energy.

Appreciate life—family, home, friends, weather.

Be organized.

Be disciplined.

Always make lemonade from life's lemons.

I read my goals daily to remind myself of what I wanted to do and who I wanted to be. My goals were the steering wheel of my life, and now was no time to change that trajectory.

When the biopsy of the mass determined CNS lymphoma, Dr. Nayak had explained the cancer and detailed its normal treatment protocols. It didn't matter, really. I already knew I wasn't going to follow a typical schedule for any disease. That's my personality, who I am: a non-conformist and a fighter.

I wanted to face head-on whatever it entailed. With my family at my side. And I wanted them to know that fun and life weren't over for them or me, no matter the diagnosis, no matter the clutch of the disease. Because I quickly realized my family was more devastated even than I was, I wanted in the worst way to give them hope.

How might I do that?

Within a week, I conjured up and planned a celebratory party at our local bowling alley—Union Lanes in Holbrook, Massachusetts, a central location for my family. I sent out emails to my immediate family and a few best friends. My sons and wife thought I was crazy to waste money at a time when we would likely need every penny.

It didn't matter. I plowed ahead, renting the entire bowling alley for the occasion.

When we arrived, the kids stole the show. There was so much break-free energy! Seventeen-year-old grand-twins Cam and Chloe, along with their cousin, two-year-old Little Evan, threw balls recklessly—although not intentionally—across lanes. The *Do Not Lob Balls* sign might as well have been written in Greek.

Awkward women dueled their less-svelte counterparts. None of us would win a bowling competition that night.

Laughter filled every corner.

Serious conversations were off limits. Our family had trudged—almost sleepwalked—through the prior three weeks. This night was about fun. Oh, and we had so much fun. They gave me hope. They found hope, too.

I held a secret most people don't understand: symbols are powerful. Positive energy matters. Bowling became the symbol of our attitude as we confronted cancer. There was something about throwing balls and bouncing pins that simply felt … right. I'm sure any psychologist reading this would have a field day, but I refused to run from cancer.

On the contrary, I was undaunted. The obstacles in front of us would be smashed out of the way like bowling pins from a perfect strike.

My five-year old grandson D3 watched his dad fist pump after a five-pin first throw. "Yeah!" He shouted in delight and jumped off his seat rabbit-fast. Grabbing a ball, D3 pushed it down the lane. The wrong lane. When it wasn't his turn.

No one cared!

We couldn't explain that we each got three chances. D3 bowled on everyone's lanes. All the chances were his.

Lessons Learned

- Positive attitude, humor, and fun allowed my family to relax and take a break from the disease. Talk about others' lives, not what is consuming your own.

- *She* stole my balance and aim; I lost every match I played against the ladies. I was awful—but it was hilarious. Laugh hard. Laugh often.

- Make fun part of the cure.

- Find delightful ways to restore balance.

- Set goals.

Questions Begging Answers

- I know I'm the luckiest son-of-a-bitch in the world. Lucky, except for the fog a brain tumor injected into my head, now making me partially blind, and asking, "When will the fog clear?"

- How can we all keep each other healthy in the upcoming months and years?

- Is this the last time I bowl?

- Will this be the last season I witness?

- How will I react to the chemotherapy?

Chapter 12

PREPARE FOR POISONING

*Just when the caterpillar thought
its life was over, it began to fly.*
— Unknown

Timeline: July 2018

I was awash in chemicals. They kept me alive and tried to kill me at the same time.

At least She isn't so bipolar. Her only intent is to destroy me. Somehow, killing her host—me—seems counterproductive.

I had paid my dues to get into the posh, seventh-floor—expensive and exclusive—cancer club. Like some sort of big-city discotheque, members were lined up. Dying to enter.

Once there, I enjoyed cocktails of methotrexate and rituximab, topped off with a shot of leucovorin, a boilermaker of sorts. Getting high on those drugs eventually caused my hair to fall out.

The first couple of treatments had few observable physical side effects. Long before Covid-19 became the monster it is, my first accommodation was to become accustomed to being surrounded by people clad in masks and gloves.

No one was afraid of catching cancer. It's not a cold or a virus. Yet everyone—patients, family, staff—wore protective gear to protect all the patients. Now that nearly everyone sports masks, we hardly notice. But at that time, seeing masks made me feel older, frailer. Frailer than I was.

At least, in the beginning.

My chemotherapy routine quickly intruded and established a new rhythm to our days.

We arrived at Brigham and Women's Hospital, located a parking spot somewhere in the five-story underground parking garage, memorized our slot number …. no, that didn't happen. I couldn't remember *any* numbers or directions. Susan remembered or wrote it down.

Later, too much later, we learned to snap a picture on our phones of parking sites, the wing, the floor, and even the elevator numbers. Multiple elevators serviced the labyrinth of joined buildings, which had been renovated, enlarged, and restructured over decades from when the hospital assimilated in 1980 from the original Boston Women's and the two Brigham hospitals.

With these handy new tricks (I needed lots), we more easily navigated a return to our car at the end of my many visits.

The first few visits were little more than extended one-night stands of one to four or more days. With all that happened during each chemotherapy installment—new rooms, new nurses, new doctors, new treatments—I barely remembered, and most times couldn't recall at all, how to get back to the parking garage.

Of all the things this fantastic hospital did, the poorly labeled trek from parking to intake to treatment was the most inefficient. It was a maze befitting the first ancient Greek puzzle-makers.

The one redeeming feature of this peculiar hospital layout was the entire staff who, without exception in my experience, graciously went out of their ways to give directions or serve as escorts to your exact destination.

After visiting my vampire friends for IV lines, I headed either to a lower floor for a not-so-favorite, character-building MRI, or straight up to chemotherapy.

After a quick pulse, blood pressure, and weight check, I was whisked off to another floor, sometimes with a gorgeous view of the Boston skyline. In each section were multiple beds separated by drawn curtains. Each time I got acquainted with an on-duty nurse who plugged me into the treatment *du jour*.

Potent chemicals were labeled with skull and crossbones on pale brown plastic bags hanging from a wheeled tripod. Some days multiple bags of goodies were inserted in my arms. The nurse-of-the-day adjusted small valves on each bag to a desired length of time.

Drip, drip, drip.

Sometimes a bag took five hours or more to empty. One tedious drop at a time.

"Mr. Kelley, is there anything I can get you before I check on my other patients?" asked the nurse as she closed the curtain closed behind her.

"No, I'm fine."

"How about a warm blanket?"

I shook my head wearily. "No, thank you."

"Just call if you need help with the bathroom."

Each "suite" of beds had several bathrooms in the adjacent halls, a troubling journey. So troubling, in fact, I wished I hadn't drunk anything before coming. But that wasn't possible. The deadly therapy designed to reach my brain also cascaded through my blood and renal systems, destroying them, too. To dilute their unwanted effects in those areas of my body not specifically targeted, I was required to drink as much water as I could manage each day. I forced down several quarts—in addition to the IV fluids flooding me.

That translated to many troublesome trips to the toilet.

I'd pull off the sheets covering my legs, unweave the spaghetti tubing, find my slippers somewhere off the edge of my bed, grab my trusty three-wheeled-solution-hanging pole, "Joe," and slowly shuffle toward the bathroom all while pushing Joe a foot ahead of me.

Once I caught the tubes on a doorknob and had to quickly grab Joe, who stumbled and threatened to crash and splash the deadly chemicals onto the floor. The noise sent the otherwise pleasant nurse running to my rescue while delivering a harsh rebuke for not asking her for help.

I valued my independence but was slowly losing it. With each new treatment designed to beat cancer into submission, I became weaker and less able to do things for myself.

A television offered passive entertainment in the suite, but daytime TV wasn't my thing. I couldn't read books; *She* had taken care of that. I couldn't focus enough to tell a one-dollar bill from a ten, not that I needed any cash there.

Bored, I counted the drips, one at a time.

Several hours into each treatment, the toxic treatment took its toll and I usually drifted to sleep. Over time, miserable mouth sores developed. Then alternating shivers and sweats in bed.

Finally—mercifully—the bags would empty. Always detail-oriented (a mighty skill for an advocate to own), Susan filled in her notes for the day, carefully recording how many bags and which chemicals I had absorbed into my veins on that round.

Time to go home, back through the labyrinth.

"Do you need a wheelchair today, Mr. Kelley?"

My answer was always the same. "No. I'm fine."

Most often, I dozed on the drive home, trusting Susan (who I began to appreciate as an exceptional driver—despite my small criticisms in the past) to deal with the heavy traffic on her own.

By now, I could no longer drive. In fact, Susan and my sons hid the keys to my truck. I was pissed! I couldn't blame them, though. They were doing exactly as I had taught them: safety first.

Yet I was convinced I could drive. That I could re-energize in the moment.

Now, with the wide-spreading rash across my abdomen causing me to twist and adjust, I struggled to find a comfortable position for the hour drive home. I eyed Susan's capable hands on the steering wheel.

I want my independence again. I want to drive!

My eyes drifted shut, but not before I made a solemn vow to myself: *I will drive again.*

Chapter 12

With all of these time-consuming trips for treatment, I was MIA at work. People in our inner circle, friends, and tenants were asking more questions. I knew we would have to tell our associates and friends; it was the message we had been avoiding.

Lessons Learned

- Cancer treatments require tremendous amounts of time.

- Patience truly is a virtue.

- As you wear down from treatments, let others step up to the plate.

Questions Begging Answers

- How much more information sharing should we do?

- How much is too much information?

- When will I get to drive my truck again?

Chapter 13

STARING
AT DEATH

You become a changed person when you face the Reaper and deny him your soul.
— MARTHA SWEENEY

Timeline: July 2018

M y cancer's form—an inoperable tumor in my brain—was here to stay. Inoperable, as in no-operation-could-remove-this-tumor.

And, like a bad tenant, She ain't paying rent.

I was all about eviction. I'd do whatever it took, whatever my doctors told me would work best.

I neither like nor want Her perched high in my brain, controlling my life.

A mere ten years ago, in a less-developed part of the world with less-informed doctors, my condition would have led to painful and certain death. How lucky I was to have such great resources! I found myself in a time and place with a better chance. Well, kind of ... sort of?

It wasn't a sure bet.

But I could still laugh at myself and at my situation. As the Grim Reaper perched on the bench next to me, I elbowed him occasionally to let him know that he sucked at his job. I was still here, present and accounted for.

If I could talk directly to him, I would mock him. "Do they have unemployment benefits for Reapers? Maybe there will be a stimulus package for you?"

Who replaces him when his job performance is bad?

What kind of resume would his replacement need?

Is there a degree called Dream-Killing?

What's the tuition to learn how to shatter lives?

I wondered how well the Reaper would handle *his* demise after someone scared the bejesus out of him.

What's it like when he is in a bad mood?

I also wondered if others shared my morbid musings or whether these were my own peculiarities.

You might think I show false bravado when I make light of death, as if it is easy to stare into death's eyes. It isn't. You have to get used to it, become dull to it. You can't *not* get used to it. It's there. Brain cancer places your full attention on death.

Death is simple. Because controlling death is beyond our reach, we choose to make it complex. We use prayer and ritual, money and resources, as if our actions alone have power to change the outcome. Most times they can't. When it's our time to go, the Grim Reaper will win.

We can explore every option with all our energy to keep The Reaper at bay. I know I do. But we don't have the final say. That's why I joke about it. Much better to laugh than to cry about what you can't control.

You can lie about death, but you can't undo it, make it up, or change it. Its truth is pure.

It's not a stretch to realize the odds are against you with a disease like mine. Ever present in this Theatre of the Absurd is the question of what to do with those the-clock-is-ticking-fast feelings. How do you bundle those emotions and present them to yourself, your family, and your friends?

My stepson Dave's wife, Michelle (really more of a precious daughter-in-love to us), and their children live with Susan and me in our multi-generational home. Michelle's outward recognition and internal acceptance of my condition reassured me that she had a reasonable grasp of the situation.

During my first hospitalization for chemotherapy, she came to me filled with concern, worried about me and about her children's reaction to my cancer. We wondered together what she should tell five-year-old Dave (D3) and eight-year-old Elle.

Michelle hoped to eliminate—or at least reduce—the issue of bad things happening in the presence of the kids. She thought they were too young to learn about the thorny side of life. Naturally, she wanted to shield them. She also didn't want to lose me. She didn't want her kids, my "stinky brats," to be psychologically damaged from losing their grandfather.

Dealing with death is hard. Some think it's even harder with young children, but it's not. Kids are tougher than we realize. Take that to the bank!

Michelle didn't want them to feel that life is hopeless in the face of diseases like cancer. I thought she should know what to tell *herself*—before telling the brats.

"You need to find a way that … it's okay that it's not going to be okay. That's the puzzle you alone can solve for you."

She sipped on the thought for a time.

In America, where every child gets a trophy, win or lose, and welfare is a staple regardless of the reasons for extending societal generosity, we've lost our ability to tell it like it is.

Michelle needed to realize that it's okay that it's not going to be okay. This was our reality now, the kids' reality, too.

Granted, it is tough to tell it like it is. Cancer doctors deal with that every day. When you discuss death by cancer or being disabled by cancer, the hardest thing is to figure out how to make the best of something quite awful. There is no easy acceptance.

We must accept the unacceptable. When *She* slaps us in the face, rudely wakes us to reality, no one can tell us exactly how to make sense of it. Some people use religion, others temporarily booze or drug their way through.

I find ways to make the present more important than thinking about the future. I'm not spending today's chips on tomorrow's game of chance. I try to enjoy life to the fullest. A friend of mine encourages, "Make every day amazing." It's great advice!

Two years after my advice to Michelle, we sat on our porch chatting about the children. Michelle admitted how much that small piece of advice helped her. She had needed to master the dilemma of playing out a bad hand. All of us need to most effectively play the cards we're dealt.

My son Phil handled the situation with humor. When people

asked how I was doing, he told people not to worry. "My dad is like a cockroach. You can't kill him."

I burst into laughter when I first heard him say that. No offense to cockroaches.

Admittedly, I've paused to wonder whether Phil is kicking the can down the road or not picking it up at all. In the end, it doesn't matter what I think. Humor is his tool of choice. Maybe it's enough to take the pressure off, until things change.

Pathways light themselves up. Endings become obvious.

Most often, I pushed back a haunting image of cancer's fast track to an abrupt end by finding activities to keep me busy. Staring at the end didn't help. Instead I did more and thought less.

I think surviving cancer is about self-control and attitude— until science catches up. *She* has had quite a head start on modern medicine.

Like perishable fruit on the counter at the grocery store, *all* of us are going bad, just at different rates. *She* accelerates the process and puts her foot on the pedal to speed up our downward slide.

A great attitude acts as a brake to slow the downhill process. A positive disposition enhances our self-control, our wherewithal to shove cancer from the driver's seat.

I believe, and there is some science to support my theory, that my outlook and positive thinking kicks cancer's foot off the gas pedal.

Admittedly, the science of cancer leads the way. We rely on our doctors. I am lucky to have terrific medical professionals who steer and oversee my recovery. Funnily enough, even from them I never get a straight answer when I ask about my prognosis. It's not because they aren't straight shooters or they enjoy sending mixed messages.

Their job is a ten on the tough-job scale. If there is bad news, no one wants to be the one to tell you what you need to hear. It's not fun.

Like so many other cancers they encounter, doctors can't predict the performance or outcome of my particular disease. Researchers don't yet know what causes CNS lymphoma. I can only imagine how hard it is to give such threatening and incomplete news to a patient.

If it were me in the doctor's seat, I'd worry whether the patient has the mental strength to push through. I'd worry that people often misinterpret or cherry-pick information, even if I did a great job explaining. I'd worry that what I said might tilt the patient's view in a way to take off the mental edge a patient needs to pull off a miraculous recovery.

My friend Judy, who worked as a hospital nurse on an oncology floor for thirty-five years, still remembers a patient who had a sign above her bed: *Expect a miracle.* That hope-filled mental projection gave her many reprieves from a serious diagnosis.

Often, things we don't understand are connected in ways we can't see. What appears to contradict is actually connected.

I have my own mantra: *you can believe in a future that you don't know and can't prove.* This point of view allows me to be both logical and irrational at the same time.

Yes, irrational logic exists.

While reading about cancer, I came across an article, "Surviving Cancer Without the Positive Thinking," by Peggy Orenstein, about Elizabeth Williams. Bravo to Peggy and Elizabeth!

What is the science on positive thinking? The article suggests positive thinking has less to do with outcomes than I think. I'm not saying I agree.

Elizabeth's candor, transparency, and depth give us a difficult-to-counter opinion that science is the cure. Peggy and Elizabeth's angle on cancer deserves a shout-out. In partial contrast to Elizabeth's view, I believe a successful outcome occurs when science walks down the aisle on the arm of positive attitude. My science-averse gut tells me assessing your individual situation correctly is the key.

I definitely know what I think impacts how I'm able to keep myself mentally upright in my cancer journey. There is no room for depression. Depression is the anti-work pill. Fight it! Saving yourself from cancer requires work, boatloads of work. My work ethic definitely helped overcome the treatments. I rely on my hopeful attitude to balance my thinking and my life.

With a focus on positivity, I can better sort out my priorities, process information, and energize myself to perform the necessary steps in my battle with cancer.

I'm still not sure whether my attitude controls how I think or whether how I think controls my attitude.

I do know a woe-is-me outlook falls far short of an effective plan. Negativity and pity parties won't help me fight the disease, make my life better, or cure my cancer.

Lessons Learned

- Your outlook affects your emotional and physical health.
- Dealing with death is difficult.
- Kids are stronger than we think.
- Positivity is a strength worth cultivating.

Questions Begging Answers

- Can I trust the science behind my therapy?
- Will I ever get a straight answer about my prognosis?
- Can I maintain a hopeful outlook?

Chapter 14

TOUR DE CHEMO

*It is the unknown around the corner
that turns my wheels.*
— HEINZ STÜCKE,
LONG-DISTANCE TOURING CYCLIST

Timeline: July 2018

With the next round of chemotherapy, I was hospitalized again. By now, my decision about how and what to communicate seemed more obvious: I wanted to be fully transparent with friends and colleagues.

Earlier, when I was first diagnosed, it seemed there was no good news, no accurate or reliable ... or definite ... information to share. No one knew the trajectory of the tumor in my head.

Gradually, as we learned more, I was able to understand more. And I felt a desire to communicate more intimately.

But how?

Never a sit-still type of person, I'd always been fidgety. I'd have been labeled with ADHD (attention-deficit hyperactivity disorder) if I were in school now.

Yet here I sat at the hospital, IV lines cobwebbed around and into me. My eyes followed the drips as they traversed the tube and dribbled into my arm.

Luckily for me, I have a high tolerance for pain.

Most construction guys do. We lift heavy objects, tweak our backs, fall off ladders, get stung by bees, endure countless splinters, lose fingernails as the result of rushed hammering at the end of long workdays. We get used to pain.

Who knew all that would stand me in good stead now? What a great baseline.

I grinned and winked at a passing nurse. Nurses and phlebotomists got a break with me. Most patients tense and cringe, but needles don't affect me much at all—the polar opposite of how I react to MRIs. I often joked with the vampires who drew my blood, in an effort to make the best of the situation.

So I found my entertainment whenever and wherever I could.

Which is why I was—initially—delighted when Dave set up my laptop at the hospital so I could stay in touch with my family and businesses.

Based on prior visits, I really didn't expect to use it for any length of time while the treatments were underway. Due to the damage *She* inflicted and more from the treatments, my eyes couldn't focus well at all. My attention span and interest level were low. My memory was worse than ever. My body was beat up and tired in spite of my determination to fight back.

On top of that, when I looked at the keyboard, it was like scrambled eggs and made no sense at all. I sighed and set aside my laptop.

Instead I turned on the TV and started watching the Tour de France. These twenty-one-day bike races were held in the spring and summer in France, Spain, and Italy. In Europe, Australia, England, and many countries, the tours were the equivalent to American football. Only the best athletes could compete.

Chapter 14

In the world bike tours, the best cyclists compete and ride approximately 2,100 miles in twenty-four days to determine the best teams, the strongest mountain climbers, the fastest sprinters, and the best new riders.

The Tour de France in biking is the equivalent of the Super Bowl in American football. Like American football, which has approximately sixteen regular season games followed by five weeks of playoffs, the races have twenty-one mini-events, or races.

Each stage of the Tour de France has a winner. Additionally the stages are combined with race times for a cumulative total to determine the final winner of the tour: the general classification winner or GC winner.

Each year the Tour grips the public's attention as gladiators of the sport compete. Country champions, world champions, and Olympic champions make up the field. It is a prestigious accomplishment to win races of this magnitude. Millions of fans around the globe follow the tours each year.

As I watched the Tour De France, my thoughts roamed. I wistfully dreamt of crossing the finish line in glory, arms raised in triumph. I was the wannabe now. But an idea sprouted from my meanderings.

What if I let people know how I'm doing by using the computer?

By syncing my progress with the twenty-one-day stage format of the tours, I could send weekly email updates to friends, family, and business associates.

Maybe I can use the Tour de France as my prototype?

I called my updates "Tour de Chemo Stages" and congratulated myself for coming up with a great way to communicate *and* alleviate the ever-present boredom permeating my hospital room.

I powered up my trusty laptop, determined to plow through my deficits and type a few insightful emails.

Subject: My Tour de Chemo

Sent Week 4, Stage 4 Report

SK, CNS

Hi, Everyone:

Hope this email finds you all feeling as great as I do. This morning (July 9, 2018), I'm at Brigham and Women's Hospital on the Dana-Farber Cancer Institute's floor for the next round of chemotherapy. Love that potent Methotrexate as it is knocking the crap out of the CNS Lymphoma.

Referees have the scorecard at SK's (Steve Kelley's) Chemo 148 to 111 CNS Lymphoma in the 4th Round. Both sides are throwing heavy body blows, but SK has deflected and ducked away from any head hits. Anyone aware of my sports playing-style knows that body blows don't matter.

The fight is going SK's and Dana-Farber's way. As we go right to the action, the chemo corner is dousing SK with IV fluids to help heal the kidney damage caused by the cancer drugs. SK is holding up well, looking forward to the next round. Reporters from the SK corner are telling us that all those years of roofing in the heat and all the mountain biking are proving to be SK's trump cards ... with apologies to those of you who aren't happy with trump cards.

It's not President Trump's fault. The game of Bridge

and its "trump" cards were invented long before The Donald's time.

For you history buffs, the trump card is derived from the 17th Century card game Whist, in vogue among the English nobility of the time. In Whist, 4 players (who comprise two partnerships) are each dealt thirteen cards from a 52-card deck, with a partnership's objective to win as many tricks as possible. "Trumping" is considered good—if you want to win.

For those of you who remain upset, we can call it the *rump* card instead.

Back to the action:

SK, in his corner said, "I will win this battle, and I have great news for my fans! I'm negotiating sponsor rights with Coca Cola for a new energy drink called Trexaid Cola. The ad campaign slogan is: *Get Strong. Fight Cancer. And live to talk about it!* We'll make a Clint Eastwood-style commercial with the line, "You want to get lucky, kid? Try Trexaid!"

SK's Prognosis: There is an unverified whisper about a complete, long-term recovery. My thoughts on prognosis: With luck, even though the actual prognosis average, according to sources on the internet, is 3-5 years (or 6-10 years, depending on your source), I'm going to beat those bastards too!!! Ha, Ha!

If we get really lucky, the doctors think there is a possibility of eliminating the cancer altogether. "You'd have to have a brain tumor to believe that one!"

If it can be done, I want to be the one who sets the record for recovery and does it. Statistics show that recurrence happens in more than 50% of those treated so my goal is to kick that too! My statistics (the ones that count) on the other hand, say that I will live to be a pain in all your asses for a long time!

No worries on my present condition. Saturday afternoon I played an hour-long Whiffle Ball game with the family and kicked butt. (Thanks Dave, D3, and Elle).

And, on August 1, the doctors will tell me whether I can mountain bike. Cross your fingers. (Note that I already cheated once and my wife and the doctors all had a hissy fit.)

Also note that my vision has returned to 97%+ in my left eye. That Methotrexate chemo is "serious shit," as my sister Mary says. And I'm glad I can be treated by it. I have the CD Marker-20 Protein, which is the luck-changer. It's a shamrock up my butt that allows the Rituxan chemotherapy to work on this particular CNS Lymphoma.

Primary Lymphoma of the Central Nervous System. Only 3 in 1 Million get it. And I'm one of the fortunate 3. Even fewer than those are treatable. I hit the lottery with the CD-20 Protein. I'm not 100% sure on that number, but, after all, I have brain cancer for Christ's sake; give me a break.

There is an ongoing problem with my kidney functions from chemo, but we are working on that, too.

I also have mild amnesia, which works wonders around my wife: "Honey, sorry I forgot _____ ." (You fill in the blank.)

And I can't navigate well. But I'll do fine if I drive with navigation, which provides me with a great excuse to buy a brand new truck!

All in all, I'm in great shape. I can almost guarantee that if you didn't know I have CNS Lymphoma, you wouldn't know when you see me. I will continue to back that up. Yikes—bold of me, but that's how it's going to be!

Love you all and definitely expect to be here in 2028 ... in 10 years. At which point, there will be a big party!

Lastly, I'm putting the plans together for the 2nd Recovery 2019 bowling party—probably August 8th or 15th—at Union Bowling in Holbrook. I'll keep you posted.

I will also send out another update mid-way through the upcoming treatment. It will probably look like this: "I'm felling grat. U should try it!" or some such version that makes me look drunk.

Lots of love and laughs to all of you,

SK

Remember: Take care of the little things, and the big things will take care of themselves! Thank you for being part of my recovery team!

Subject: SK Status Update for Team

Sent 7/25/2018

SK, CNS

Hi, Everyone:

Hope you are all well.

For those of you who don't know, my favorite sporting event is the *Tour De France*, which coincidentally starts every year around my birthday (July 7th). The top bike riders from all over the world ride 2500+ miles through France and occasionally dip into Spain, Germany, Switzerland, and Italy over 21 days. (Each day is called a "stage.")

Riders compete for best climber, overall best rider, best

sprinter, best team, and even most aggressive rider. People throughout the world love the excitement and drama of the Tour de France. Before, during, and after each stage, there is enough drama to produce a real-life soap opera, much like my own Tour de Chemo.

Just to get to today's Stage 5 of SK's Tour de Chemo at Dana-Farber in Boston, I was rushed out the door this morning by Team SK's chief strategist and captain Susan Break-Your-Balls DeBalsi.

"What's the rush?" I complain.

"Shuddup and get in da car," she ordered.

I comply. She has a real mean streak, as most of you know. So we get to the hospital in Boston inordinately early, and they lock me away (again) for more chemo; this will be Methotrexate treatment #4.

Now, I'm not complaining but I knew something was funny on Floor 7B. I couldn't figure it out at first. Hmmmm. All I could think of was, "Why was Susan in such a hurry to get here?"

Then it hit me like a brick. All the nurses on this floor are men. And they are all good looking, mostly Italian. Susan is Italian, in case you couldn't guess. Now just as I am writing this, I begin to wonder, "What else is in that Methotrexate? Do I still like football? Have I been enjoying that Olympic figure skating too much?"

Come to think of it, maybe we'll keep an eye on the TV to see the *Giro d'Italia*, the first race of the three each year. If I'm really lucky, maybe we'll break the bank—if I can get out of here—and take Susan to Italy. Biking Italy! Yeah, That's a dream. Boy, this Methotrexate is strong!

Looking forward, SK's Tour de Chemo, Stages 5-8, will run through Saturday. Like any good soap opera, there is marital strife and gender questioning (or answering).

Family vacation St. Maarten
JULY 2009

Steve competing in the Jersey Devil triathlon
APRIL 1, 2017

Happy to be
on a roof
NOVEMBER 1, 2017

My doctors said, "Don't worry
about side effects!" Hmmm!?
SEPTEMBER 1, 2018

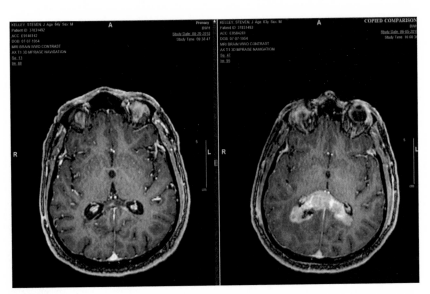

The growing hidden tumor threat
JUNE 1, 2018

Prepped for stem
cell transplant
NOVEMBER 19, 2018

Kepivance
baby face
DECEMBER 5, 2018

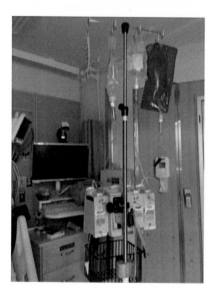

Methotrexate
to the rescue
JUNE 2018

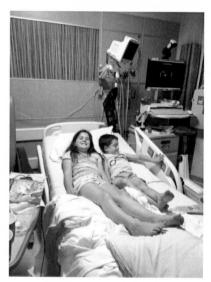

Stinky brats need
treatment too
JULY 2018

The "Big Boss"
at my side
DECEMBER 2018

Take my hair!
I don't care! I'm alive!
JANUARY 1, 2019

Mountain bike madness
OCTOBER 10, 2020

Dr. Tim Smith, my neurologist and brain surgeon, just met with Susan and I. He asked rather incredulously, "What could you possibly have done to deserve this woman?"

Susan is in heaven now! She thinks this surgeon is great. She is surrounded by men who either love her, fear her ... or are Italian.

You can't make this up.

Lots of love and laughs to all of you,

SK

Remember: Take care of the little things, and the big things will take care of themselves! Thank you for being part of my recovery team!

Lessons Learned

- Writing can be a great pastime and a lot of fun.
- Emails are a life-saving connection to the outside world.
- Self-entertainment is a vital life skill.

Questions Begging Answers

- Can my cancer be completely eradicated?
- What is the next step to return to normalcy?
- How do other people handle all these invasive treatments? Especially kids?

Chapter 15

CALL IN THE TROOPS

She stood in the storm, and when the wind did not blow her way, she adjusted her sails.
— ELIZABETH EDWARDS

Yet another MRI (which still had the power to make me cower) indicated the multiple doses of methotrexate and rituximab and cytarabine over the summer had temporarily arrested the mass in my brain. *She* had stopped growing, had even shrunk back in alarm at the strength of the ammunition used against *Her*.

Now, I faced decisions about long-term survival with no way of knowing how much control I might have over the end result. That was all right. With my cancer team, I had found a way to get through the first phase of this difficult disease. I was good—for now. We'd continue to take it one step at a time.

It shouldn't go unmentioned that my brain wasn't at full capacity.

My doctors knew the neuro-pathways that route my thoughts had been damaged. My forgetfulness, vision problems, and inability to concentrate were obvious to me and to my family. But we were at a crossroads: if we stopped treatments now, with just the initial rounds of chemotherapy completed, I would very likely experience recurrence in the near future.

A recurrence I might not be able to reverse.

Chemo drugs are incredibly strong, and my energy had depleted with each round of treatment. Connections in my brain severed or melted away from the toxicity.

The process had not gone wrong. On the contrary, my tumor and the connecting arteries and nerves were shrinking. Yet I couldn't tell if I was improving or regressing. Doctors said my condition was stable.

Stable.

What does stable mean? I had no way of knowing.

Recent MRIs, they told me, confirmed the tumor was no longer visible on its scans.

What does that mean, no longer visible? Do I still have cancer?

Doctors were cautious, saying little about a long-term prognosis. I sensed they knew more than they were telling me. They did.

Primary CNS lymphoma's recurrence rate after a patient's initial chemotherapy is high—over 50%.

If we stopped treatment at this point, I'd be rolling the dice on my future with a bad bet in a low-odds game. I knew *She* had set up shop in my head. Thanks to methotrexate, rituximab, and cytarabine, we walled *Her* in; *She* still controlled lots of my brain function. *She* controlled my life, not me.

When I looked at numbers or dates, I routinely missed the first digit: 1990 looked like 990; $2,500.00 looked like $ 500.00 on a computer.

But why?

Who knew? I certainly didn't.

Not that I complained. I knew how lucky I was. The good news was that with chemotherapy, there had been steady, if slow, improvement of brain function, and I worked through many vision-related mistakes.

With the help of my sons Dave and Phil, I managed to participate in our business enterprises. I learned to double and triple check everything until I got it right. In the office, I passed most of my estimating and writing work to others for review. No harm, no foul.

My sons, staff, and friends pointed out any mistakes they caught. I conceded and corrected the errors and moved on. It was okay if I missed a few things, erred a bit. That's why God invented the delete key and the eraser.

I am alive. That's what matters. Self-validation and reassurance were a constant in my thought processes, and I continued to stake out my claim on a positive outlook.

Still, I had my worries. And questions, so many plaguing questions.

Will CNS go away for good?

How long will I live? My doctors can't say.

More importantly, how healthy will I be for the time I have left?

Can I have a good life with Her lurking inside of me?

As impertinent as it sounds, I wondered whether I truly could have fun again.

Will my life be normal?

No. It wouldn't. Deep down I knew that. My family knew it, too.

But my medical team had another trick up their sleeves. They offered a daring plan.

Later in August at the behest of Dr. Nayak, my good-natured physician assistant Aleks introduced Susan and me to Dr. Ann LaCasce. We met on the cancer floor of the hospital in Dr. LaCasce's office to discuss additional treatments. I felt nervous.

Why do I need "additional" treatments? Didn't the chemotherapy work? Why do we need more troops?

The news was a small blow.

Susan looked nervously at our new soldier in the war against cancer. Well, she wasn't actually a soldier. Dr. LaCasce's take-charge demeanor made it clear from the beginning: she was a general, not one of the troops. She would control the tactics we'd use, the strategy to further disable and denigrate my primary CNS lymphoma, our savage opponent.

Dr. LaCasce's goal? To disarm lymphoma completely. To make *Her* fully impotent.

General LaCasce was an expert at a specialized type of warfare: stem cell transplants. She explained that, without the transplant, I would wait for cancer's inevitable return to my brain.

I took a long breath and exhaled quietly, not quite sure what to think of the new reality she presented.

Before my bout with cancer, I honestly knew little about lymphoma. I had no idea what a stem cell transplant was. I came to understand that an autologous stem cell transplant—the best fit for me, according to General LaCasce—is, in its simplest form, multiple, heavy doses of chemotherapy poisons.

Dr. LaCasce, along with Dr. Nayak and Aleks, did their best to explain the procedure. They shared a vision of a difficult-to-undergo treatment tunnel, which, upon exiting at the other end, would potentially give me a new lease on life.

No guarantees, though.

If I agreed, we would begin testing and prepare for a November assault. The treatment would not involve donors.

I would use my own blood cells, hence the descriptive word autologous. What would the cells do? How would they do whatever it was they were supposed to do?

General LaCasce explained that her campaign would require poisoning my body to the fullest extent possible without killing me. The procedure involved removing my blood and fortifying it before reintroducing it back into my system. The intense chemotherapy drugs would have done their dirty work and killed most of my tumor.

At first, Susan and I didn't know what to think. If the procedure went badly, I would be no better off. I might be even be sicker than before. Worst case, I might die.

As a non-medical person, with no small amount of past brain trauma, I was being asked to drink out of a fire hydrant of advanced science with a straw in place of the barrel-sized hose I needed to digest our battle plan.

General LaCasce posited that stem cell transplant was the best choice for a return to the vibrant life I had led. She suggested we sleep on it before giving our answer.

That night, Susan and I researched stem cell transplants. She called her medical friends and our good friend Dr. Weinreb, my PCP.

There wasn't a fully convincing, safe-for-me argument for either of our choices. It was a typical catch-22. Damned if you don't try it. And quite possibly damaged if you do. I had to make up my mind by morning.

General LaCasce had more than hinted at side effects: diarrhea, vomiting, rashes, hair loss, quarantine, mouth sores. Pandora's box was next.

Go for it! I want the whole enchilada.

I want to get this monkey off my back.

I'm not living in fear only to look back and wish I had taken the best chance for the great life I wanted.

Contrary to logic, I made the unsettling, near-death pieces of my situation not matter. This wasn't a fairy tale. There was no tooth fairy. I couldn't change my situation. I couldn't wish it away.

What I *could* do was focus more than ever before on life's simple joys, joys like bike rides and sunrises. With determination, I built positivity into my life each day. I chased away negativity in favor of focusing on best outcomes.

Lessons Learned

- By now, I have a love-hate (strong on the hate) relationship with MRIs.

- Don't trust your own comprehension skills.

- Advocates are vital to help you navigate the slew of information thrown your way.

- At times, what you don't know is more powerful than what you know. (Einstein gave us that hint.)

Questions Begging Answers

- How soon will medicine provide doctors and patients the ability to fight cancer without all the dangerous side effects we experience today?

- How much more damage can *She* instigate?

- Can I gain precious time by lengthening the fight with my demonic foe?

- Can I sway the fight in my favor?

- Will *She* metastasize to other parts of my body if I don't do the transplant?

Chapter 16

IN THE RING WITH MY CANCER TEAM

*If you even dream of beating me
you'd better wake up and apologize.*
— MUHAMMAD ALI

The Grim Reaper was doing his job and he punched hard.

Thankfully, it wasn't only me against him. I had a team of doctors—including General LaCasce—working to beat the cancer. Once started on the stem cell transplant path, we knew we would be sparring with the disease as if we were in the first rounds of a boxing match, where punches and counter-punches are thrown to get reactions. In my case, side effects and tumor size.

The latest MRI delineated the tumor's reduced size, which kept the Reaper sulking and scheming while we strategized.

Results were positive, but I'd taken a few shots to the head. Now ever present was "chemo brain," a euphemism to explain away the confusion attributed to patients undergoing chemotherapy. In spite of my team's explanations, I couldn't make sense of my status. I was … disoriented.

Cancer patients get confused from chemotherapy regardless of where the cancer is found in their bodies. Like anyone experiencing such difficult treatments, I had no baseline, no prior experience, to measure against. I couldn't tell how I was doing. I struggled with the information provided in my corner of the ring. I didn't know how the judges viewed this fight.

My ability to think was deeply impacted.

The brain is your command center, your interpreter of the outside world. Its job is to make sense of the inputs from your environment, process them, then direct your responses. Only, mine wasn't working well at all. I was fighting like hell to think, but I had a glass jaw.

Brain cancer prevented me from reasoning well, even without chemotherapy. It can't be overstated: I was easily confused. I had a sinking feeling as I realized I couldn't grasp anything complicated. In my head, I was playing checkers while everyone else was playing chess.

My doctors, my wife, my son Dave explained ... and re-explained ... everything to me multiple times during the weeks we waited for the new treatment I would undergo. Gradually, I came to partially understand the impact stem cell transplant would have on me and on my entire family.

A patient in my situation must decide whether to play it safe or aggressively attack cancer. Playing it safe has a greater risk of disease recurrence. Aggressive treatment dilutes the risk of recurrence, but doesn't eliminate the risk.

My best option, everyone assured me, appeared to be an autologous stem cell transplant. This option had the potential of decreasing the cancer's chance of recurrence 20-30%. Initially, this sounded optimistic. In hindsight, was it really logical to endure so much for a 70-80% likelihood my cancer *will* return?

That's as good as it gets? Even with the treatments? I was devastated.

After your car dies on the freeway, if you could finagle a 25% chance that your car wouldn't shut down again, would you work really hard for that? I'm not sure. You'd probably buy a new car.

Sadly, I couldn't buy a new brain. I had to work with what I owned.

Prior to the stem cell procedure, I learned, the doctors would harvest my blood after giving me Granix—a man-made, protein-boosting hormone that stimulates infection-fighting white blood cells. Stem cell transplant de facto kills everything in your blood. The doctors use complex formulas to bring your body and systems to a complete standstill.

My weight, reactions to drugs, and my body's ability to produce white blood cells to help regain my natural chemical balance all factored into my corner's strategy as we probed cancer's defenses.

General LaCasce, the transplant specialist, bolstered my confidence with her stern approach as she outlined the schedule for our counter-punches.

"We'll use thiotepa, busulfan, and Cytoxan. These are powerful drugs, Steve."

"What are they?" I asked, as though my foggy mind could make sense of the upcoming regimen. My question was a fool's errand and she knew it.

"We've done this regimen frequently, Steve."

Even so, I had my private concerns. "Can I stop treatment if I'm not doing well?"

She slid right past my question, instead assuring me, "You'll do great!"

But I wasn't done. "What's the worst that can happen?"

Well, that was the wrong question! she as much as said, with a scornful grimace.

"What are my chances?"

Another semi-pantomime look told me there would be no good answer forthcoming. Her schedule was tight. Her patience had run thin.

But, wait a minute; there truly was a catch.

Of course there's a catch. There's always a catch.

The procedure might be worse than the disease. It can kill, especially if you get pneumonia or other illnesses during treatment.

You have to pay to play. You must be a risk-taker.

The doctors did their best to educate my family and me about risks and rewards, pains, and gains. The risks were sky-high. The rewards might be high, too, but they came with multiple catches. I wanted so desperately to have my life back. To think clearly. To ride my mountain bike. To be home with my family instead of being in the hospital.

Should I take the chance?

We decided stem cell transplant was the best option on the table to push *you-know-who* out of the eagle's nest.

"Research shows that long-term results are best achieved with additional, potent chemotherapy poisons." Dr. LaCasce's gaze was serious, steady. "Those poisons will also cause damage to your kidneys, lungs, skin, and the rest of your body."

The potentially severe side effects to kidneys and lungs require close monitoring during the operation, she told us.

Military operations have a name for this. They call it collateral damage. I grimaced at my dark humor.

My immunity against infections and disease, she explained, would be destroyed, making me susceptible to polio, measles, chicken pox, pneumonia, and other life-threatening ailments.

"It will take two years to recover," Dr. LaCasce warned. "And that's *if* all goes according to plan."

We all knew things rarely go according to plan.

Will my transplant be smooth? I could only hope.

Based on cases of brave patients before me, doctors—using the best science available—prescribed this same regimen of aggressive drugs. Even more toxic than my earlier rounds of chemotherapy.

The Reaper was clicking his heels and cackling. I ignored his menacing taunts as we prepared to ramp up treatments. The risk was substantial.

The ultimate risk. The thought haunted me.

I saw it was my next step to recovery. And I was willing to go out swinging.

Lessons Learned

- A stem cell transplant is not a sure bet.

- Sometimes, you need to take the ultimate risk—against all odds—and pray you'll live to see the reward.

- Be willing to finish the fight.

Questions Begging Answers

- How long before I feel like myself again?

- CNS lymphoma has a great fight record. Will I win this bet against the odds?

Chapter 17

FUN AND (DEADLY) GAMES

A person without a sense of humor is like
a wagon without springs. It's jolted
by every pebble on the road.
— HENRY WARD BEECHER

Timeline: October 14, 2018

To be eligible for a stem cell transplant, my cancer had to be in remission. To this end, Dr. Nayak's team had prescribed six intravenous treatments of rituximab, five of methotrexate, and two of cytarabine over a period of several months. The drugs had done their jobs. *She* shrank to a barely noticeable amount on my MRI scans.

Each drug had had different, uncomfortable side effects. The worst for me was cytarabine—what I called CyTerrible.

CyTerrible made my lungs feel as though they were coated with molasses. I couldn't take deep enough breaths to be comfortable when I exercised. I felt hypoxic and exhausted.

Some of the IV treatments lasted a day, others five to seven (necessitating hospital stays). Generally, each individual treatment required about eight hours to transfuse the chemicals into my blood.

Not everyone is a candidate for the stem cell transplant I faced. Its harsh side effects can kill you. I needed to be cleared or approved for the risk. Before we could move forward, a crazy amount of tests needed to be done. In spite of the seriousness of the disease, I maintained my sense of humor. Below is my unapproved version of the tests they insisted I endure.

To understand those tests, you'll need to conquer the annoying and incessant use of acronyms in the medical field, including AMA—which might stand for American Medical Association or leaving a hospital Against Medical Advice.

PPD: You are injected with tuberculosis. If you survive, you get to move forward. If not, you can go home. No more medical bills to worry about.

PFT: This pulmonary test includes a marvelous hypnotist named Jaoull, who convinces you to take deep breaths of a mysterious, un-named smoke (sadly, it's not a joint) while sitting in an air-tight, glass-paneled machine. Jaoull has his own testing room at the hospital. After inhaling as much as you can, you blow out the smoke into a plastic bag. The machine measures the smoke. I scored 134% on the exhale portion of the test, an exceptional number.

CXR: They take a chest X-ray to determine whether any of Jaoull's funny smoke was left in your lungs.

CBC: During these draws, Dracula runs a daily Halloween party at Dana-Farber along with nineteen friends—each needing a vial of my blood. I know the number, because that's how many vials of blood they sucked from me in two days. Blood markers for anemia, electrolytes, hemoglobin, and liver function are recorded.

One of the IV lines spilled blood onto my pants. The nurse was upset. I felt bad for her, so I gave her some of my medical marijuana. She was very happy, especially afterward.

IV: This is a highly stylized method to steal your blood.

It takes skilled nurses just minutes to insert the line. It took me several days to learn how to spell intravenous.

BMT: This informative session delivers information on bone morrow transplants. But it is actually a thinly veiled, documents-signing opportunity to release the hospital from liability. Including Jaoull's funny-smoke test.

TBFT: For this testicle balance and fertility test, my testicles were placed in a giant centrifuge (because … that's what was needed for the job) and spun around. Wheee! Okay, I admit I made this one up.

In reality, the specific gravity of the testicles is used to determine when the stem cell treatment can begin, and what my before-and-after-chemo fertility is. Apparently, the hospital wants to make sure I (at age sixty-four) don't threaten the world's population balance with multiple children from accidental leakage of sperm.

HDB: This test counts the density of hair follicles prior to surgery and assesses the shape of the skull by flipping a bowl of Jell-O onto your head. After two minutes, the bowl is removed, and the impression indicates exactly how much polish I will need to buy for a lifetime of baldness.

My good friend Bob Mendillo will finally be satisfied as my dome will be as shiny as his (and my son Phil's, and my stepson Dave's).

EKG: Specially trained nurses place electrical leads on your chest so they can take out their frustrations on male patients by ripping the hair off the men's chests as they remove the electrical leads. And, of course, all the while they purr, "Oh, does that hurt? I'm so sorry!"

AIC: What I fondly call The Money Grab, this is a behind-the-scenes affordability and insurance test. Essentially, it plays out like this: No insurance? No money? No stem cell! Funny, not funny. Fortunately, I passed; unfortunately, many others don't.

At the end of the day, I was finally through the roll call of what felt like unending exams. The science and data suggested I had a reasonable chance of surviving stem cell transplant. But, as you might guess, the doctors had difficulty when it came time to assess my mental health!

Fully approved for the transplant, I needed to decide whether *I* was fully on board with moving forward.

Am I? Am I totally committed?

Doctors had already introduced us to the science of stem cell transplants and presented us with options and survival percentages. I went from being lost at the onset of cancer, to being lost in science, to analyzing life and death risks with my half-at-best capacity brain.

Tolerance for risk plays an important part in a patient's transplant decision. Still reeling from chemotherapy and losses to my brain function, the risk factors had been difficult to grasp.

There I stood, knee-deep in the quicksand of CNS lymphoma. My choices were: a) ramp up the treatment or b) leave things as they were in the hopes the cancer would desist. After all, *She* had shrunk dramatically and, with any luck, wouldn't dare decide to get aggressive.

I took a second long look at the major, life-altering transplant.

This is no movie; this is life. I swallowed hard. My *life*.

I'm playing Russian roulette for real now, and each chamber of the gun is loaded.

My decision was a crapshoot, any way I looked at it.

Even if stem cell transplant is the lifeline, it's still up to me to grab the rope ... and then pull the trigger.

My cheeks puffed as I expelled the deep breath I'd been holding.

Okay, then. Let's get started!

The autologous stem cell transplant, I learned, would kick off with a short surgery to install a port, a plastic valve to enable infusions of the drugs. I didn't like the idea of adding synthetic parts to my chest; it was another get-used-to-it moment.

A necessity, of course, but unwanted.

Just accept it and move on, Steve, I told myself. *This is a drop in the bucket compared to what's ahead.*

Lessons Learned

- Hospitals converse in a unique language.
- Learn to speak it.
- It's wise to keep your sense of humor, especially on rough days.
- Multiple medical tests prove I'm ready for stem cell transplant.

Questions Begging Answers

- Does port surgery require another damn MRI?
- Stem cell transplant is high-risk. Am I up to the task, strong enough to withstand the onslaught?

Chapter 18

PREPARING FOR BATTLE

When you are going through hell, keep going.
— WINSTON CHURCHILL

Timeline: November 19, 2018

With or without the transplant procedure, *She* was a life-threatening force. But in conjunction with my medical team, our calculated guess suggested that transplant was the pathway to a more forgiving future and the least likelihood of early termination.

How odd to frame the end of my life with the word termination. My life isn't an employment contract to be severed for poor performance.

I prepared myself for a tough battle. Even though I didn't like the catabolic energy of punitive thoughts toward cancer, the battle metaphor fit. It was definitely going to be a fight. There would be a victor, a victor at the expense of the vanquished.

From what my doctors said, I surmised the battle would be like trench warfare in old world war movies on the big screen. One side pitted against the other.

On my side, I needed to prepare for sickness, diarrhea, vomiting, delirium, skin rashes, itching, and swelling. That was a cocktail of crap I certainly didn't want.

A cancer crap cocktail. I'd rather have a beer.

C'est la vie. Get used to it, I laughed to myself. After all, what can you do but laugh?

I got ready for what would, hopefully, be a temporary loss of mobility. Sitting still was tough for me; lying around tethered to yet more IV lines had the effect of putting me on a leash. A leash? A leash was anathema to my personality and positive outlook. I feared IV lines. A balloon doesn't do well once punctured. I didn't like the whole puncture-and-seal-back-up-again idea for my body.

And the first puncture was next on their agenda.

A different, but related team did my port surgery. Cutting into your arteries is a serious undertaking. Even so, I was in a good mood when they wheeled me into surgery.

"Hey, Doc, are you sure I'm in the right room?"

"Yeah, at least I think so," someone retorted. A guy wearing a headlamp chortled.

As the cold room sank into me, I shivered and glanced at the bustling nurses busy setting out assorted medical tools.

I cleared my throat to get their attention. "My wife told me I am getting an operation." I paused for effect. "Surgery for ... you know ... for an *enlargement*."

"Are you sure I'm in the right place?"

The room abruptly stilled.

The nurses eyed each other. They eyed the doctors. They eyed me. And, for a split second, uncertainty hung in the air.

Everyone burst out laughing.

"Sure wish *my* husband would consider that operation!" one of the nurses chimed.

I grinned as the room dimmed and I drifted off to sleep.

My personal M.A.S.H. team successfully attached the tubes that would be used to administer drugs into my chest. Going forward, whether I needed saline, medication, or my own blood (freshly run through the centrifuge machine), it would be the site of choice for injection.

I roused from the surgery with my new normal confusion of not knowing where I was. A nurse attended me as my limited awareness returned. I found all the nurses at Dana-Farber Cancer Institute well-trained in these unique, life-saving procedures. Each encounter filled me with gratitude for their professionalism and dedication.

Even knowing its benefits, I found the port completely unappealing. Having valves attached to my inner organs and protruding from my skin felt creepy. Like I was the human experiment in a Frankenstein movie.

I awoke to a new friend at my side: another three-wheeled bag-hanger. My pole buddy would accompany me everywhere. It would transport the toxic chemicals, blood, and medicine that flowed in and out the tubes of my port during the transplant procedure.

Port in place, I was ready to take on the chemicals designed to search and destroy the tumor.

Lessons Learned

- Don't hesitate to make others laugh.
- During battle, the human body can endure even the most unsavory assaults.
- A port is convenient for drugs and blood infusions, a terrific weapon in the arsenal.

Questions Begging Answers

- Can I stay positive throughout the stem cell transplant?
- Who is being poisoned, *Her* or … me?
- What will be my collateral damage?

Chapter 19

GREASE THE SKIDS!

An ounce of action is worth a ton of theory.
— RALPH WALDO EMERSON

Timeline: November 2018

As I began the next phase of treatments, some of my physical strength surrendered to the chemotherapy and stem cell drugs, despite my vow to maintain as much vigor as I could. The procedure would last five to eight months—in and out of the hospital—and I dreaded a huge deficit in vitality.

During my first extended hospital stay, I petitioned doctors for a stationary bike to ride while being treated. It was an unusual request. Most people treated with intensive chemotherapy are not able to exercise. You end up flat on your back, barely able to move. Luckily, due to my conditioning, I could still ride the stationary bike—or I assumed I could.

I wanted to give it a try.

My regular exercise routine entailed two hours a day. With the advance of cancer and ensuing treatments, my balance wasn't reliable. The medical team feared I'd fall off the bike and pull out the IV lines. I knew they felt conflicted because they wanted my spirits high.

Cautiously and somewhat begrudgingly, the team accommodated me. So I climbed onto the bike intermittently for two to three hours each day. The staff managed to work around the bike as they treated me, changed sheets, and took my daily vitals.

Often, I'd quietly grind away in the middle of the night. Nurses poked their heads in the door and grinned. They admired my determination to remain active. At the same time, I was a novelty, totally unlike their typical patients. More often than not, they gave me you-are-crazy looks.

When I first arrived on the floor, I wasn't offered the opportunity to get a bike. Stem cell transplant patients don't usually have the energy. Often cancer patients bottom out throughout treatment and recovery.

On the other floors where I had been treated earlier in my cancer journey, patients in better shape requested a bike upon arrival. If the doctor approved the request, staff was instructed to follow through. A minimum three-day delay; three days without exercise. While attached to an IV in my isolated room, I was stuck with nothing to do. The delay and idleness drove me crazy.

When my doctor arrived, I asked for a bike. I even offered to have my own brought in. He agreeably ordered the bike but warned it would take some time. My visits lasted two to ten days for treatments.

At each succeeding admission I requested a bike. Always delivered by a physical therapist, the bike couldn't be ridden without a mandatory assessment and training to ensure patient safety.

Over time, I befriended the physical therapy team. By now I was a frequent flyer on the cancer treatment floors at Dana-Farber. Every few weeks when someone courteously and quickly delivered a bike, I had Dunkin' Donuts gift cards waiting for them.

With a PT's assistance, I learned the system and how to get in an early queue for a coveted stationary bike by emailing ahead to let them know the timing of my next visit. This ensured a bike reserved in my name. Success!

Even so, protocol required its dues be paid.

After each admission, I still had to request a bike from the attending doctor upon arrival in the CNS lymphoma unit. On one occasion, the doctor gave his standard spiel of a three-day timeline. As he spoke, we heard a knock at my door. (Doors are always kept shut on transplant floors to contain germ spread.)

My friends on the PT team pushed a bike into the room. The doctor did a double take and looked in bewilderment at the miracle he'd witnessed.

I grinned at his confusion.

The seriousness of well-trained staff was evident with the restrictions on family visits, handling chemicals, and the food. Anyone sentenced to our quarantined wing couldn't eat anything that tasted good.

My friend Robert always said if food tasted good, then it was bad for you. If it tasted bad, then it was good for you. Wouldn't you know, the good-for-you food was the only thing allowed on my diet.

The menu included mainly boiled or frozen-then-boiled items. No fresh vegetables at all. No milk. No *anything* with even a hint of bacteria. I consumed sterilized food that made shoe leather seem like a gourmet meal.

I wondered if the angriest members of the staff voted for this food. I was certain science was behind all of it. Right?

GREASE THE SKIDS!

Yeah, right.

The science of cancer treatment is truly amazing. Doctors and scientists are capable of destroying all of the blood cells that relate to cancer in order to control cancer's growth. The side effects are dramatic and can be life threatening. Those of us in treatment become test subjects for this fledgling and uncertain science.

Considering the options, we have little choice. Personally, I was grateful for the opportunity to live and be part of this great stem cell experiment. I was lucky to have a branch of hope extended by dedicated professionals at the forefront of medical science.

That didn't mean the journey was easy.

Lessons Learned

- Rules ... *rule*. Be creative to achieve and satisfy your needs.

- Make friends with staff members. They might be your key to comfort.

Questions Begging Answers

- What else can I do to make my hospitalizations more tolerable?

- Can I continue to plow through a system that doesn't recognize me as an individual?

Chapter 20

ENDURING
THE CURE

There are poisons that blind you,
and poisons that open your eyes.
— AUGUST STRINDBERG

Timeline: November 2018

*H*ospitalized again. I sighed in resignation.

During July and August alone, I had been in the hospital for thirty-three days. Now, I settled into Room 12 on the sixth floor (dedicated strictly to transplant patients), with no one except immediate family allowed. About twelve other lucky candidates were locked away, too, each of us approved for life-saving stem cell procedures. We had no contact with the outside world or each other, quarantined as we were in our individual bubble spaces. Many were so sick from the chemotherapy drugs they had no interest in talking to anyone, anyway.

Several patients never lifted their heads off their pillows. The stem cell transplant wreaked havoc on their internal organs, the poison leaving them nauseous around the clock.

Two sets of vacuum-sealed doors with electronic card-key access, plus a person standing guard, prohibited anyone without clearance from entering—insurance against germs. All of us were immuno-compromised.

Sixth floor nurses were fantastic at their jobs. So many soldiers armed with swords of empathy: Nori, Carol, Karen, and too many others to mention.

In addition to my earlier chemotherapy using methotrexate and rituximab, my team prescribed three well-known cancer-fighting drugs to counter the brain tumor. Busulfan, thiotepa, and Cytoxan—all with proven capabilities to pass through the blood-brain barrier. Once through the sac that protected my brain, the chemicals could work their destructive magic.

The treatments were ... unbelievable. How doctors keep you alive and poison you at the same time is an act of artful finesse.

During my first regimen of IV drugs, the bags suspended on tripod poles looked harmless enough. Nurses, wrapped in plastic protective garb, were careful not to spill or touch the harsh toxins. With good reason.

I earned my own respect for the drugs. Within days, I noticed puffiness in my cheeks. My throat constricted. I decided to make the difficult journey to the bathroom for a look.

The treatments were draining; my fatigue was bone deep. I climbed out of bed, guarded the IV lines, and shoved the tripod ahead of me as sweat beaded my forehead.

No wonder curiosity killed the cat. It's doing a number on me!

When I got to the bathroom and peered at myself, I didn't recognize the fat-face guy in the mirror.

Who is this miserable looking cuss?

I was startled at my marshmallow cheeks, at my ripe swollen lips. My soccer ball-sized face. My gums protruded, larger than life and certainly larger than my teeth when I smiled. Smiled? You bet I did. I was quite the sight.

I was never more thankful to be a man. The women in my life had always taken greater pride in their appearance than I. This thing staring back at me? It would have frightened away a hungry pack of wolves.

Somehow, I had transformed into The Hulk. I wasn't green yet, but I didn't doubt it could be coming.

Perhaps this is just a preview?

I steeled myself for the coming slew of disturbing side effects predicted by my cancer team. I had what seemed like unending diarrhea with its accompanying rawness. Forty pounds of muscle and weight slid off me during the transplant.

Predictably, I waved goodbye to my hair. Unpredictably, I also said farewell to my fingernails and toenails ... and hello to an irritating purple rash all over my body.

I lost more and more memory.

Unfortunately, along the way to the brain these jarring poisons grimly affected kidneys, lungs, and soft tissues throughout my body. The most significant problem I encountered was mouth sores, which prevented me from eating or swallowing for three weeks. Not an ounce of food passed my lips due to the painful cracking each time I dared to open my mouth.

Any food that sneaked in acted like acid on the wounds. I couldn't tolerate bananas or soft fruits. Hard food couldn't be chewed; even fresh bread was too hard.

As the soft tissues in my throat swelled, my lips and cheeks bulged like a sunburn gone horribly wrong. Simple swallows of water tortured the inside of my throat.

I didn't dare let my lips drift closed so excruciating was the pain if they touched each other. I drooled constantly. I wasn't a pretty sight. Thankfully, the Yankauer—a plastic, handheld suction—came to my rescue.

Every four hours, a nurse checked my vital signs and asked me to rate my pain. A high rating (eight to ten) necessitated a dose of fentanyl. The fentanyl caused delirium.

I despised that the most.

Hallucinations plagued me. Susan and Dave witnessed a specific delusion when I thought I was in a school auditorium.

"This place is filthy," I told them. "Get it cleaned up! Look at those things hanging from the walls. I don't like it!"

Then I began to yell, "Get me out of here! Look at all the bugs, those brown bugs with their ugly antennas. They are disgusting. Gross. Please, get me out of here! Get—me—out!"

Dave leaned over my bed, trying to calm me, trying to reason with me. "Steve, listen, Steve. There are no bugs here."

"You're lying! Can't you see those bugs? They're gross—and they're everywhere! Please," I clawed at his arm, "just get me out of here."

"Steve, calm down. You're in the hospital. Mom and I are here with you. Calm down."

I tossed and turned in the bed, plastic tubes threatening to spill their lethal cargo.

In addition to the fentanyl, doctors had prescribed other medications—specifically palifermin—to decrease the torturous mouth sores caused. It only intensified the swelling. My face looked like I had been swarmed and stung by hundreds of bees.

You can imagine how three to four weeks of cancer-killing drugs, pain-managing drugs (opioids), and swelling-control drugs made life miserable. I hated the disorienting feeling of the pain drugs above all else.

To add insult to injury, I couldn't floss my teeth, not a small thing: I couldn't stand my own breath—which reeked like badly over-baked garlic. It wasn't a joy for my caretakers either.

By the third week of isolation, I lost patience. Especially for the Dilaudid and fentanyl, two opioid drugs used to control my pain. As much as my body had taken punishment, my mental status was worse than it had ever been. I couldn't tolerate any more imaginary bugs crawling the walls.

Deciding I would rather be in more pain and still be able to use what was left of my brain, I insisted on stopping the fentanyl. Staff didn't cooperate. With each incoming shift, I was asked about my ever-present pain level, and the same medication order would be reissued. Staff was compelled to follow the established protocol. I knew they couldn't be faulted, but the honeymoon was over.

Finally, unable to cope with the hallucinations that bedeviled me, I drew a line in the sand. I demanded they stop the Fentanyl or I would ... I would ... I would leave AMA! Against Medical Advice—the term medical staff use to refer to patients who leave before their treatments are complete—is discouraged at all hospitals.

As I saw it, though, I had finished the treatments. My IV lines had been removed. The remaining part of my stay was aimed at convalescence and regaining strength and stability. Granted, I was at tremendous risk for infection if I left, but I simply couldn't function with the fentanyl.

I knew I was immunocompromised, but that wouldn't change whether I was in the hospital or not. I could be equally careful at home, I reasoned, with Susan executing cleanliness protocols. She would threaten to execute anyone who didn't comply; our house would be in lockdown.

I cannot do another week of this!

I decided to cut my hospital stay short and gathered my possessions, donned my mask and gloves, and went home.

In spite of our contrary positions with my forceful exit from the hospital, I appreciated Dana-Farber Cancer Institute, where nurses seemed undisturbed by the sci-fi me that would appear after the drugs. It was always business as usual for them. I was grateful for their diligent care—and for every new minute they had added to my life.

I was eager to go home and *live* it.

Lessons Learned

- Stem cell transplant is every bit as harsh as doctors claim.

- The pain is terrible; the pain drugs are worse.

- Speak up forcefully when necessary, especially if your medical team isn't listening.

- Mouth sores *hurt*.

Questions Begging Answers

- Will I regret my decision to exit the hospital?

- With my compromised immune system, will I be safe at home?

- Will medicine evolve without all the dangerous side effects we experience today?

Chapter 21

LIFELINE OR ASSEMBLY LINE?

There are more than 9,000 billing codes for individual procedures and units of care. But there is not a single billing code for patient adherence or improvement, or for helping patients stay well.
— CLAYTON M. CHRISTENSEN

I write this chapter more carefully, more deliberately than previous ones in order to address a touchy topic. A rather sensitive topic I feel quite qualified to debate after extensive experience as a patient within the medical system.

As a lifelong manager, I know how hard it is to maintain the mission of a business. It's hard to deliver value to each client every day.

Hospital administrators must keep themselves and their teams aligned with their mission. Theirs is the difficult task of managing costs, egos, and sprawling growth in an environment of fast-changing regulations and even faster advancing medical science. Adapting to unforeseen priorities like Covid-19 complicates an already complex job.

Continuity of care is yet another issue. Hospitals employ good people who do incredible work—despite a system that gets in their way.

In my experience, hospital and medical protocols were constantly changing, speeding patients through an often-disconnected system. Nursing homes and long-term acute care (LTACs) facilities are, equally, inherently dangerous places. Even more so during these turbulent Covid-19 times.

You can deny this assessment, but you'd be spitting in the wind.

I'm aware of medicine's resistance to criticism. My criticism is harsh and completely necessary. At one point during my own journey, I left the hospital against the advice of my medical team. (See Chapter 20.) I tried hard to not step on toes, but my own toes got crunched pretty hard.

None of this takes away from how much I respect hardworking nurses, interns, doctors, PAs, aides, administrators, social workers, and other professionals who played important parts in my treatment and recovery. I especially appreciate my cancer doctors who worked with me to keep me as important as the dollars I was producing.

There are many parts to the story. The healthcare industry and its support of scientific advances are amazing. Yet corporate greed has distorted cancer treatments to a profit center—and converted patients and insurance to cash cows. You need to understand the pieces of the system that support the medical business model.

To turn a cancer diagnosis into a clean bill of health, the health care system leverages science, the medical workforce, private investments, insurance coverage, real estate, government, and publicly traded companies into a monolith that houses medical care.

Huge investments support the science, the real estate acquisitions, the equipment, and the legal protections necessary to be viable. The entire system needs to justify those investments. To get the most out of the system, you need to carefully and forcefully navigate the system.

Let's talk about the tools you'll need to overcome these obstacles and steer your recovery ship.

Among other things, you'll need:

- **A PATIENT ADVOCATE:** a competent, medically savvy, forceful person on your side.

- **A GREAT MEDICAL TEAM:** composed of reliable professionals who diagnose, plan your treatment, chart your progress, and—if you're fortunate—celebrate your successes.

- **GOOD INSURANCE:** hopefully a company that doesn't deny claims or treatments—a huge relief for patients and family members.

- **A POSITIVE KARMATIC SOUL:** someone who cares about the people caring for you.

I was lucky. My wife, a physician assistant, understood the system, its weaknesses and its strengths. She was an incredibly strong and powerful advocate in my behalf. And my insurance, Capital Blue Cross, deserves a shout-out.

When dangerous drugs are shoved into your blood, lots of mistakes can happen. As laymen unfamiliar to the system, we forget that when we are hospitalized, there are three different shifts of people within each twenty-four hour day, all of whom must communicate and coordinate our care. The ball gets dropped frequently.

In my case, medications were added that shouldn't have been. My wife would look at my patient portal and examine my medication list every day for mistakes. She found many.

Overworked and fatigued, nurses and doctors filling multiple shifts would gloss over reports that should have been read carefully, analyzed, and acted upon. Instead, the status quo of the day was simply box-checked in place of ordering or requesting the changes necessary for better treatment.

LIFELINE OR ASSEMBLY LINE?

Without an "equal-status" advocate at your side, complaints are easily ignored. One weakness inherent in the system is what I'll call the Bed-Full Syndrome. As long as the bed is full, there is a job to do. To those trudging to work each day—their personal problems presumably tucked away during their eight-hour shift—the circle opens and closes seamlessly.

The system simply wants to be fed. It doesn't care who is in the bed as long as that bed is full. Your job is to get out of the bed and out of that facility as quickly as possible. The longer you stay, the more you are at risk.

Hospitals are inherently dangerous.

Those nurses, technicians, researchers, PAs, doctors, administrators, and custodians who make miracles happen to save lives like mine deserve great respect. But we can't disregard the ever-present dangers in our system of medical treatment. More important is the danger of human frailty. As humans, we all make mistakes.

It's easy to lose sight of the power money holds in the medical field. Money powers the medical engine. That's when filling the beds matters more than the people in the beds.

When medicine becomes little more than an assembly line, it impacts quality of care.

One example: initially, Susan, acting as my patient advocate, requested the addictive fentanyl prescription be halted because it caused my debilitating hallucinations. Under its influence, I was neither functional nor rational. Yet, as each shift produced a different team, more fentanyl was prescribed. She filed countless complaints and reports. (Read the full story in Chapter 20.)

These drugs would, I deduced, kill me or wreck my spirit before the cancer did. When we couldn't effect change, I made a critical decision to dismiss myself from both the hospital and the impossible situation. I packed my things and called my wife.

I felt no guilt. I knew the bed would be filled by someone else—*stat*.

I was lucky. I broke the fentanyl curse. I didn't get hooked. In this phase, unlike the majority of my treatment, the system was counter-productive and harmful. I had to initiate change. I was respectful but determined. The teams didn't coordinate well between themselves, making coordination the weakest link in my care.

I left the hospital the next morning.

Lessons Learned

- Mission statements and finances drive medical systems.

- You have to know when to take control of your own care.

- Dare to speak up—forcefully when necessary—especially if your medical team isn't listening.

Questions Begging Answers

- Where do I go from here?
- What new threats await me?
- Can I hold them at bay?
- Is it finally time to rediscover my life?

Chapter 22

PATRON SAINTS
OF CYCLING

Bicycling is a big part of the future. It has to be.
There's something wrong with a society that drives a
car to work out in a gym.
— BILL NYE

Three months after hospitalization for the stem cell transplant, my life had inched its way back to semi-normalcy during a cold New England winter. I had conquered the transplant, won the battle.

At least, for now.

Our business was back to its regular form with Dave and Phil mostly running the show. I helped, but my sons shouldered larger roles in preparation for eventually taking over company.

My body had changed, too.

Numerous side effects had manifested in hair loss, vomiting, and weight loss, but I hadn't expected to be cold all the time. Always warm and sweaty under any condition, I was now forty pounds lighter. In response, I shivered, jacked up the heat, and even used an electric blanket for the first time, one of many unwanted adjustments.

Susan and I had a new subject to argue over. "Honey, it's too hot. Turn down the thermometer."

"Look," I tossed back, "before, whenever you were cold, I put up with the heat being on. Now it's your turn!"

Susan bit her tongue, but her expression said: *If this is the worst of it, I shouldn't bitch.*

By February, I could no longer ride my mountain bike due to snowed-in trails. As quickly as they cleared, I jumped at the chance to ride, which was nearly every morning. I dressed for the cold, and the fast-paced exercise kept me warm until I got back to the house, where I dumped my sweaty clothes in the washing machine and raced for the shower.

As my bike friends say, "We rides in all weathers!"

I ached for the exercise, ached to build back my conditioning, to enjoy the outdoors and the harsh cold air in my lungs.

Ah, I thought each icy morning, *this is truly living!*

No one felt the joy of being outside more than I did. The hospital had been a stark reminder of my mortality. Four walls, machines blinking, constant interrupted sleep for mandatory vital checks. I'd had enough.

I repeat, I'm no good at being sick.

Determined to get back into shape and fully embrace life after a two-month stem cell hospitalization—and the Grim Reaper's knock on my door—I had jumped on my stationary bike every day, but couldn't wait to break way to my real rides outdoors.

I wanted Susan to be in equally good shape. She didn't really like biking, but I convinced her to ride with me by buying her an electric bike so she could easily keep up.

I had an ulterior motive, a secret plan.

Susan had always wanted to visit Italy, and, after what we had been through, I decided we were both due a reward: a fabulous trip to Italy for my fabulous Italian wife.

If the doctors agree. And if my body cooperates.

So much hung on those conditions. Should we go? Was it too dangerous?

Am I healthy enough to make such a major trip? Will Dr. Nayak and her team greenlight the idea?

With a good deal of trepidation, I hazarded the question during my next checkup. After all, what was the worst that could happen? She could only say, "No. It's too dangerous, Steve."

Instead, Dr. Nayak centered her response on how I felt. Did I feel strong enough to travel?

Truthfully I don't like traveling. I wasn't sure how I felt.

But how long do I have? We should go for it.

I never liked travel the way Susan's friends did. After a cruise or a flight to wherever, they would tell stories laced with fantastic food choices, museums galore ... expert lectures, too.

Blech!

I didn't want to spend the money just to board a cruise ship, sit on my ass, and do nothing. Nor did I find the idea of wandering around a museum to ponder archaeological mysteries at all appealing.

But a bike tour? Now, that makes sense!

Chapter 22

Dr. Nayak said she would consult with her team.

Two days later, Aleks phoned. "Steve, we think it might be okay for you to travel. Pneumonia is a big concern, so you have to watch out for contact. No handshaking. No physical touching. You'll have to wear a mask everywhere you go. Gloves, too."

That was the answer we'd hoped for. "Fantastic, Aleks. Please let Dr. Nayak know how pleased we are."

But I wasn't as confident about the trip as I appeared to be. Fear and uncertainty hung over my head, creating a dark cloud of doubt.

Determinedly, I pressed forward to my next step of my plan. After several online inquiries, I found a couple of energetic, positive-minded accomplices: Pat and Grace Fitzpatrick, a buoyant couple from Australia, who owned International Bike Tours.

I confided that I was recovering from cancer. Did they have room for a not-quite-healthy bike enthusiast on one of their tours?

"No problem, mate," Pat said. "We'll get you on board and up to speed, Steve. I promise."

He asked a few questions about my conditioning. I readily admitted I wasn't in touring shape for the fifteen to seventy-five miles per day, but Pat said he would make adjustments each night of the tour depending on how I felt. If needed, I could even have a rest day. We could sightsee—music to Susan's ears.

What about Susan's conditioning?

Just like she had on the home trails, Susan could ride an electric bike. This was her bargain with the devil. She wasn't comfortable on bikes and certainly didn't want to be with a bunch of testosterone-bound, semi-pro wannabe bike riders.

She decided to give it a try. It was Italy, for God's sake! She had only dreamed of visiting the home country of her grandparents. She did, however, have one pressing question.

"How many women will be on the tour?"

Amazingly positive and accommodating, Pat organized a thirteen-person tour scheduled for May 22 through June 1. He said there would be two couples, including us, so ... one other woman.

One was enough.

In April, I extracted 8,000 sticky dollars from my account and made a deposit for this exciting, much anticipated, vacation-of-a-lifetime. It had been seven months since we discovered *Her*, a scanty three months after finishing the stem cell transplant.

That's a bridge with a lot of water running under it.

I hadn't recovered fully, but I was convinced I would, determined I would.

Even though Susan had never ridden more than ten miles at a time, we braced for the adventure. The tour would follow the 2019 Giro D'Italia, one of the three major world biking events I adored watching. The Giro visited near Lake Como, where we could pause at the museum of Madonna del Ghisallo, the patron saint of cycling. Passionate cyclists came from all over the world to pay their respects to past tour winners, especially to Italian cyclist Marco Pantani—*Il Pirata*—The Pirate.

His short but stellar career captured the world's attention as he raced to first-place finishes in the Giro and the Tour de France in 1998. I had read about his skyrocketing and then plummeting career, matching the same precipitous climbs and drops in the Alps, the same mountains he had assaulted to become the Italian mini-god of cycling for a too-short ten years.

Our tour would take us high in the Italian Alps, with sweeping views of pristine, ice green, mountaintop lakes. Temperatures would waver indecisively from balmy shorts weather to snowy, layered-clothing climbs.

As a special treat, we would also get to visit a business associate of mine, Gianluca Marini, and see his factory in Saronno, Italy. Gianluca and I had become friends while negotiating work on a property he owned in Massachusetts.

At one point, when my bid wasn't, shall we say, properly Italian enough for him, he shouted, "Steve, don't break a *me* da balls!"

I had laughed so hard that I caved in our negotiation—which smoothed the way for a lasting relationship.

Gianluca, his mom, and his wife would host us for a day and include a tour of his robotic-powered manufacturing plant.

On Wednesday, May 22, jittery with excitement, we boarded a Lufthansa flight from Boston to Frankfurt, Germany. From there we went to the Malpensa airport in Milan, Italy, where we connected with Pat and our tour mates.

We split into a couple of smaller groups for a forty mile ride. By now, Susan was confident on her electric bike, which was black, pedal-assisted, and Italian-made (yeah, Italian everything). It was a bit heavy for her, but otherwise quite serviceable and fast. She handily impressed the whole team, especially given her lack of experience.

Pat led our group of eight. After about ten miles, I couldn't keep up with the pace. Some of the faster riders—and my super-fast Susie on her electric bike—broke away as we went up the side of a steep mountain. Apparently in the excitement of the ride, no one noticed me lagging.

At a small intersection, they made a right turn. When I arrived at the crossroads, I kept going straight. I don't know why, other than I was pumping the pedals hard and my head was down as I tried to catch up with them. Of course, even had I known the way, I wouldn't have remembered it.

My cancer and the transplant still restricted my ability to envision maps and make road-worthy decisions.

The group stopped at a small store where, shortly, Susan noticed I was MIA. She later told me how our group waited ten minutes. How Pat, our worried tour leader, thought I should have appeared by then. Susan called my phone, hoping I had phone tower coverage. I didn't. The area was too mountainous.

Abruptly, at the point of exhaustion from an exerting climb, I looked around and discovered there was no one with me. I was by myself, a lone biker on an unfamiliar trail.

Those guys are fast! I thought. *Me, not so much.*

I found myself riding solo, deep in the woods on a thirteen-foot-wide paved road, no houses on either side. Neither did I see any pedestrians, not that it would have helped. I was alone. In Italy. And I didn't speak Italian.

Pat was upset, alarmed to discover that I hadn't downloaded the day's route. He worried that I'd panic. (He needn't have. By then, I had already decided to get over being lost. Being lost was a way of life by now. Nothing new for me.)

"Pat," Susan encouraged, "Steve's a survivor. Don't worry. He'll figure something out."

Pat shrugged off her advice and grabbed his phone to try a second time. Luckily, by then I had reached the top of my climb and had phone reception.

I was quick to answer. "Hey, Pat, is that you?"

"Ciao bene! Ciao bene, Steve."

That was, we'd learned, Pat's singular, go-to Italian phrase for everything. If he negotiated a parking spot, *"Ciao bene!"* he exclaimed. When we were stopped by police, *"Ciao bene,"* he chirped. (They let us go.)

I thought the literal translation was "hello good," but it covered more than that. It had a magical effect on everyone he interacted with, including me. How can you get mad at someone who approves of everything you say, good or bad, with *"Ciao bene"*?

"Geez, mate, what happened? Where are you?" Pat's Australian accent was thicker than ever, laden with trepidation.

"I don't know. Sorry, Pat. I couldn't keep up," I admitted. "I might've taken a wrong turn or two."

"Why didn't you download the app, mate?"

"Really? I don't know how to use that crap, Pat." I rolled my eyes. "I'm better off if I sniff out the directions like I always do."

"Ciao bene!" he responded. But the dismay in his voice slipped through. "Steve, you are in Italy!"

The intimation was there.

He thinks I'm a knucklehead to believe I could find my way around in Italy.

He wasn't wrong. That wasn't my shiniest moment.

"Steve, describe to me where you are. What do you see?"

"I'm on a hill. I went through an intersection and pedaled straight up."

"Good. I know that hill. I know where you are, mate!" His relief was palpable. "Now, bike back down to that same intersection and wait there. I'll ride over and get you."

Pat was leading a pride of lions and didn't want anyone among them to get hurt or lost, not to mention how that might reflect on his touring company and wife, Grace.

Not that he needed to worry. His talent was amazing. He melded experienced fast riders, two women—one completely inexperienced—and his own three-person team through Italy, into and out of hotels, airports, and restaurants. I've never met anyone better at juggling than Pat, a patron saint in his own right!

With the pride reunited, we biked back to our hotel, ready to enjoy a satisfying meal. The team would get to hear another folly-filled episode from their chemo-brained, knuckleheaded riding partner.

Chapter 22

As we wrapped up our daring adventure, Susan and I were eager to return home to our enjoyable routines again. Constant change took a toll on me, resulting in forgetfulness—*Where did I put my jacket?*—and confusion—*Where am I supposed to be?* Without my home computer, my days felt interrupted and disoriented.

Of course, my days are disoriented, anyway!

Lessons Learned

- A cell phone is an essential tool.

- A vacation is the perfect diversion after the trauma of cancer.

- Dreaming up and executing a big plan proves you haven't lost your mojo!

Questions Begging Answers

- Will Susan and I have the opportunity to bike tour other countries?

- Might the Tour de France be our next destination?

Chapter 23

FROM FINALE
TO FUTURE

Life isn't about waiting for the storm to pass.
It's about learning how to dance in the rain.
— VIVIAN GREENE

Timeline: February 6, 2021

Two and a half years after my cancer diagnosis and stem cell transplant, I settle into my office chair to write this final chapter to *Cancer R.I.P.* To look inward at where I've been. To express how and where I landed after treatments. To share my secret—and not-so-secret—goals for my future.

In the beginning, *She* created a tidal wave of fear, uncertainty, and overwhelming levels of decision-making. Susan and I suddenly experienced life with more vulnerability. No one wants more vulnerability. Primary central nervous system lymphoma shattered our security and threatened our vision for our future together.

We were faced with crushing new priorities as I underwent surgeries and engaged in energy-sucking chemotherapy.

She demanded attention, but I had news for her: *She* had picked the wrong guy. Sure, I had an inoperable brain tumor, but I wasn't going down easy.

After *She* threw the first punch, I threw her into a chemical pit and tried to drown her. Each time *She* came up for air, I pushed her down, drenching her in chemicals until *She* finally stopped thrashing. More importantly, *She* stopped growing and enlarging her formidable form into my brain.

Early and timely acceptance of the disease was a difficult but necessary first step to a better outcome. From the beginning, I worked hard at staying positive and building a supportive, focused team to champion my choices and progress.

When asked by a friend what he should do after his cancer diagnosis, I suggested he pause and break entirely away from the barrage of information he was receiving so he could find, focus, and work on his inner peace.

Throughout life we benefit when we *slow down*. When we stop. When we take time to breathe. A long pause allows us space to push negative energy to the back of the ride. I despise back-seat drivers. I might not be able to shut them up, but I don't allow them to sway my thoughts and actions. Their dark views fall on deaf ears. I refused to allow them into my life.

Now, after successful treatment at the Dana-Farber Cancer Institute and with help from an incredible medical team, I've been able to rebuild my life. I bask in my family's love and spend countless hours enjoying friends.

Throughout recovery, I found out I could force improvement in my brain through hard bike rides and workouts. I could *feel* my brain processing things faster as my rides accumulated. I found a sort of fountain of renewal! Plus, I love to ride, to enjoy friendships, and to rebuild my physical condition with many bike partners leading the way.

Yesterday morning, I rode eight glorious miles on my mountain bike, ate breakfast, and got ready to plan out the full day ahead. A real coup.

As of today, this very moment, my physical skills, vision, balance, and bike riding ability are almost back to a pre-cancer normal. I'm not the sharpest tool in the shed, but lots of my friends think I wasn't that sharp *before* cancer!

That's not to say I don't have my deficits. The taste of food took a nosedive from interesting to bland. My solution? Put hot sauce on eggs and spaghetti and just about everything so I can enjoy eating. Sure, I get strange looks. Who cares?

It took two months of recovery before I jumped behind the wheel to practice first in my driveway and then on a private road. When I felt confident enough, I asked Dr. Smith whether I could drive again. He posed a few questions, gave me the standard follow-my-fingers test (up and down, side to side).

I passed.

When he gave his blessing, I knew he was not only the smartest guy in the world, but also a best friend.

I worked extremely hard to relearn how to drive safely. I looked each way, not twice, but three times before I allow myself to proceed. I had to retrain my eyes and brain to cooperate.

To test my memory, I once retraced my steps in an attempt to recall where I was headed on the fatal day of my truck accident. That's when I realized memory, like freedom, is something we take for granted.

She charged after my memory with a vengeance. Within two weeks of that accident, I could no longer function normally. Even now, I fight *Her* for territory every day. *She* continues to wreak havoc in my ability to think.

Writing this, more than two years later, is tediously difficult. It requires multiple re-reads to ferret out extra letters that routinely sneak out of my keyboard and into my work. How does that happen?

It might be that I need even more naps. I succumb to a tired incompetence without frequent flyer shut-eye. Luckily, everyone in my inner circle understands.

I still lose things. Yesterday it was my gloves. Fortunately I have multiple extra pairs. As you can see, my life is a daily adventure, but I'm feeling my way through it.

I still sometimes get things backward, so my sense of direction is often skewed. This morning's episode of "Let's Confuse Steve" occurred on the way to a snowplowing job. I inexplicably decided to find a new shortcut.

Shortcut? Not by a long shot.

Instead, I drove directly into an old comedy. "Oh, no, Mr. Bill. Don't do it!"

I finally "found" my way by begging my phone to "take me to Allen Street Braintree."

But that's okay because the deficits are balanced by my sense of humor, which is much improved. I'll trade laughing on a journey that's become longer any day for arriving on time wearing a frown.

A surprise gain: My hair grew back, a full mane. It has a softer texture than before—and, no small miracle, is no longer white! It returned as a pleasant sandy brown. At the time of stem cell transplant, I would have loved to know this trade-off was even a possibility. Why didn't General LaCasce tell me that in our first discussions? She ought to be court-martialed for dereliction of hair duty!

And did I mention memory? I've lost mine! Just as my son, Phil, arrived today to swap trucks in order to do a job with a smaller plow. He complained, "Dad, you left the window down. There's snow on the seat!"

"Hey, Phil, I've got a brain tumor," I cajoled. "What do you want from me, anyway?"

He shook his head, groaned with an appreciative level of understanding, and laughed. Now that's a perk not many people have: a get-out-of-jail-free card for almost everything. And boy does that little excuse get a workout.

One more unexpected bonus at this stage: a return to writing has lifted a weight off my shoulders. As I capture my cancer experience on paper, I feel how it heals me. I hope it offers the same to others.

I've saved the best news for last: marital ... um ... bliss still works!

Because those fighting through their own cancer nightmares often ask, I would be remiss not to include some helpful thoughts.

My most easily given but difficult-to-apply advice? Two words: adjust quickly.

How, you ask?

Your new reality requires your acceptance of the diagnosis.

Grieving your losses is part of your journey. Don't deny grief. Yet understand that grieving is a snare from which you must quickly escape. As you (or a loved one) fight cancer, the place you ultimately arrive at depends on how quickly you focus your energy to re-balance your life.

Deliberately re-ignite and nurture your natural survival instincts. Battle cancer. Force your body and your brain to work harder.

Nurture and battle don't seem to mix. You have to do both. Balance is key.

Use what I call your "karmatic soul," the place from which you draw your ability and desire to care for others. Even if you are the one with cancer, cancer shouldn't prohibit you from self-nurture.

My hard-won pragmatism from years of owning my own business suggests that if there is nothing you can do to change a situation, focus on making the best of it.

Be like the expert seamstress who gives life to torn fabrics, making worn pieces better with patches that are stronger than the original fabric. You, too, can make the patches of your chemotherapy be your strongest parts.

Be like the welder whose scar-shaped "j" beads painstakingly join broken steel parts. You, too, can make your recovery scars your strongest parts.

Be like the software designer whose second and third generation patches make the product far superior to the original design. You, too, can patch your broken life to become its strongest yet.

How you handle your cancer challenge will set the trajectory of your life—and the lives of your family and friends. It's important you get it right. Throw yourself into the fight.

There are incredible, hope-filled advances in treatments including T-cell and gene regeneration therapies. I hope my story can be part of your positive thinking as you re-focus your life on your best outcome using positive energy!

SIX CRITICAL TASKS CONFRONT
ANYONE WHO ENGAGES CANCER:

- Accept without submission

- Grieve without becoming a victim

- Protect your family

- Re-establish natural survival instincts

- Re-balance your life

- Create new goals to re-envision your life

You can, with your cancer team, make your own miracle happen! What are you waiting for? Get to work!

Now, as I look ahead ....

What? That surprises you? That I'm forward-thinking? That I'm planning a future? It shouldn't. Sure, cancer tests you. *She* is a formidable adversary. *She* knocked me down. But I got back up.

She doesn't force you to stop hoping and believing. You are in charge of your own mindset.

Once, when I lived for a while on the beach, a terrible storm came and cast lifeless lobsters onto the sand. I collected them in a bucket of seawater to save for a cookout. The next day, I phoned some friends.

"Free lobsters. Come on over!"

When they arrived, the motionless lobsters of twenty-four hours earlier were miraculously alive and crawling all over each other in the bucket.

Does *She* have that kind of tenacity, the ability to survive even a powerful chemical storm? I hope not, but if *She* does try to come back, I'm up for another round. I am determined to slay *Her*!

You should never throw the first punch unless you know your victim will go down and stay down. You have to finish the job. I'm finishing the chore of finishing *Her* off. Maybe I sound awful, and vicious, too. I'm okay with that because it is an attitude necessary to my survival. I need to punch and counter-punch simply to stay alive.

Speaking from my experience of recovering and living with primary central nervous system lymphoma—which has, to quote medical journals, a "dismal" outlook—I continue to believe in my recovery. While science isn't perfect by a long stretch, I have benefited from incredible breakthroughs in cancer treatment. (I'm hoping you will, as well.) In addition, new treatments and therapies are on the horizon.

With a firm belief in recovery, I continue to take heart. I focus *ahead*, on what I want to see happen. To that end, I use every tool at my disposal.

I take heart.

I stay positive.

I hold tight to hope.

I place my faith in miracles.

I practice restorative meditation.

I fight cancer with every drug available, with every fiber of my body.

I invite cancer to flow *out* of my body to find alternate energy to cancel *Herself.* I tell *Her,* "There is something out there for you. Find something to cancel you, so you don't harm the world." My goals: Push cancer out. Shut *Her* down.

My full focus is recovery.

I never forget that in a split second, in a tornado, in an unexpected accident, or an illness, all of what is really important can be snatched away.

I practice gratitude. I'm thankful beyond what people can understand for the precious extra time added to my "ticket" after it was punched by cancer. With my new lease on life, every day matters. *Every* day. Rainy afternoons are a joy. Snow is a blizzard of fun. Scorching sun is a spa-worthy tan waiting to happen. Each new day is a chance to gulp in deep, cleansing breaths that expand my thinking.

Never take breathing for granted. *Not* breathing is an indicator of a different outcome!

With an inoperable brain tumor, I might easily, selfishly ruin today by worrying about tomorrow. Instead, I postulate, "If you are going to be miserable, you might as well be happy about it."

My theory?

See the grandchildren. Stay in shape. Live in the moment. Spend time with friends. Help family members. Help others. Enjoy life. Volunteer! Bike! Go to the beach, twice a day! Don't look over your shoulder—look ahead.

Now, if only I can remember where I left my keys, my glasses, my mask, my flashlight, and my wallet, I can get on with my day ....

No matter. I breathe deeply with hard-earned joy.

Miracles *do* happen. I know: *I am one.*

Lessons Learned

- Family is important.
- Deficiencies are uncomfortable. Deal with them.
- Don't sweat the small stuff.
- Everything is small stuff!

Questions Begging Answers

- Will my insurance continue to cover my deficiencies?
- Will any new deficiencies develop?
- What can I do to help others dealing with cancer?
- Is it possible that I am truly recovered?

Chapter 24

SAINTS AND ANGELS

*Sometimes the most productive
thing you can do is rest
and let your angels wrap you in their loving wings.
They've got you covered.*
— ANNA TAYLOR

A s I wrote *Cancer R.I.P.*, I recognized that my side was only half the story.

The many saints and angels in my life made my recovery possible, so here I include some of their accounts of kindnesses, sacrifice, and searches for answers.

They share what was going on in their worlds while I struggled to survive and reconcile my new life with CNS lymphoma. Amazingly, they supported me while maintaining their own responsibilities throughout my journey. I'm indebted to them all.

Perhaps their stories will help you through the difficult times in your personal journey through cancer?

These are my personal Saints and Angels:

I'm thankful to have a beautiful, devoted sister in my life. Here is her story.

While Steve was in the hospital going through chemotherapy and stem cell transplant treatments, I called him every morning at 5:00 a.m. when I woke up. He and I would cry and talk.

We shared stories about our siblings, parents, spouses, children, jobs, and lives. In short, we got to know each other better than ever before. Most people grow up, move out of their childhood home, and establish a newly independent life. It's really hard to connect deeply with your siblings and family.

I wouldn't call Steve's cancer a blessing, but what word better describes the grace, intimacy, and forgiveness we now share with each other?

You can only touch people this deeply in times like this.

My advice is to cherish the moment. Don't shrink from it. It will build strength in your journey together.

— Mary Helmuth

My two incredible sons, Phil and Dave, have made me the proudest father and brought so much joy to my life.

Looking back on the last several years and our family's cancer journey, we'd like to share two lessons that have stuck with us. First, work is far more powerful than worry. Second, if you don't have a positive mindset, you are unlikely to have a positive outcome.

When our dad was first diagnosed with cancer, we felt like we were hit by a freight train. It happened so fast. We had known something wasn't right, of course. He was having trouble reading architectural plans, working with numbers, and managing simple navigation, all of which normally came as naturally to him as riding a bike.

We had hoped it was something simple, like cataracts,

but we were not so lucky. Instead, not only were we dealing with the dreaded "c" word, but it was a serious variant called primary CNS lymphoma.

Without treatment, it was likely our dad would be dead in less than two months. In a matter of days we went from a happy, fun-loving, hard-working, (mostly?) normal family to a family in crisis.

We were in shock.

Dealing with the trauma of diagnosis is important. When you're told that your loved one is about to go through hell, and that chances are high you'll lose them in the process, it is an emotionally violent experience.

We had already gone through that process once, a few years prior, when we lost our mother to cancer. There was a lot of crying, confusion, and fear. We felt small and powerless—mere pawns at the mercy of the gods and the vast institution (and bureaucracy) of modern medicine.

Processing the diagnosis was the first major hurdle on this journey. After we had recovered from the shock of the moment, we found ourselves wondering ... what do we do now? We could bury ourselves in a mountain of worries, or we could get to work.

We knew that worrying about things beyond our control would do us no good, so we chose to tackle what we *could* control. We had a family business to keep running. We dug in and worked hard to minimize the impact of our dad's absence.

Each of us in the family carved out roles—a sort of family care plan, not for the cancer, but for the human. My dad's sister, Mary, was his morning confidant. She played an important role in caring for a person who rarely slept past 4 or 5 a.m. and was not prone to hospital living.

My dad's wife, Susan, acted as his personal medical advocate, putting her years of expertise working in medicine into effect to hold each practitioner to the highest possible standard of care.

Susan's son, Dave, and his wife, Michelle, supported Susan at home.

We ran the business and distracted Dad with news from our business. We all arranged a myriad of trips to the hospital, working in shifts to keep his mind engaged and his spirits lifted.

Our network of friends and allies proved crucial. Dad's work friends, like Tom and Dave at Beacon, Mark and Scott at Murphy Coal, and contractors like Gary, our electrician, and Wes, our plumber, all picked up the slack.

Dad's bike friends were amazing, too. Luis, Shawn, Luke, and David pulled him up and down bike trails with incredible patience.

They all helped us as we progressed through Dad's treatment regimen. It was truly a team effort. It took everything we had.

Even with all we were doing, it was far from enough. Despite the lack of direct proof, we are convinced that our dad's survival was not just a result of the powerful chemotherapies and treatments that were administered with expert medical guidance, but also his incredibly positive attitude and the mindset that he would defeat whatever came his way.

At first, he too was overcome with the prognosis and the gravity of the situation. Whatever doubts and fear he had, they controlled him for perhaps the first week of his diagnosis. After that, cancer (and everyone else) had best get out of his way. He had a life to live and a family to lead, and CNS lymphoma was not going to stop him.

Within two weeks of Dad's diagnosis, he was already planning his first cancer recovery celebration—a bowling party for over 50 friends and relatives to celebrate his recovery from cancer. To be clear, at that point he had just started his treatment plan and survival was not only uncertain, it was unlikely.

Within a month of diagnosis, we had the first recovery celebration, which was a smashing success and triumph of family leadership. A second event was in the works. Positive energy pervaded his thinking throughout his often arduous and sometimes debilitating treatment.

For months we spent our time celebrating the good and working through the bad. For him, the end result was never in doubt, at least not in any meaningful way. He taught us all that you have a chance to overcome any challenge—if you put your whole mind and heart to the task and are willing to get to work.

— Phil Costa and Dave Kelley

If I'd had a daughter, I hope she would be as positive as my stepdaughter-in-law, Michelle, the cheerful pill I'm privileged to take each day I see her.

Going through cancer with a loved one is a roller coaster ride of emotions. Highs and lows. Dips and twists. You need to buckle up, never knowing when those dips or twists are right around the corner.

Savor the highs, work through the lows. Warm embraces, encouraging and difficult conversations, laughter, exercise, meditation, long deep breaths—whatever it takes to get you through those tough moments.

At the lowest of lows—when we were almost positive Steve was not going to beat cancer, he looked right into my eyes and spoke the most powerful words anyone has ever said to me: "You need to be okay when things are not going to be okay."

Sometimes, knowing what to do is the hardest thing. What a life lesson!

It took a while for that to settle in. I had to find a way for my mind to encircle this fleeting, hard-to-grasp concept. I had to soak in it and soak it in before I understood. That was Steve's precious gift to me. Pay attention, I told myself.

Keep in mind, he was the one not sure of his time left here on Earth, yet somehow he was still taking care of me.

I felt so lucky to mirror his energy. If you can be that kind of a mirror for those around you, you'll make it through.

— Michelle Dubois

I leaned often on my strong, reliable, determined, and dedicated stepson, Dave – who stands tall next to my son, Phil.

Before his cancer, Steve and my mother built an in-law apartment attached to their home and opened their existing four-bedroom house for our family to move in.

Steve and Mom took the in-law apartment; my wife and I took the house. We all took a chance.

My wife and I moved in with our two "stinky brats"—Steve's love-soaked nickname for his grandkids.

We happened on the perfect dream. Mom and Steve are terrific grandparents, and our kids love them. Steve and I became great friends, respectful of each other's wit and grit. Everything was terrific, better than any of us had expected.

Then Steve got CNS lymphoma.

As an IT professional in the medical field, I researched his cancer and spoke to friends and doctors in my inner circle, quickly learning how serious this was. We went from a dream family scenario to a nightmare in a matter of days.

Steve and I had spent hours in conversation on leadership, his favorite topic second only to mountain biking. Learning and knowing what to do when there is no one there to tell you what to do was Steve's definition of leadership.

At first I didn't know what to do, but I had no choice but to lead. Here is what I'd like you to know:

My natural reaction is always to assume everything is going to be fine. It's a defense mechanism that didn't work this time. A defense mechanism that couldn't change Steve's cancer. My kids, wife, and I had to deal directly with this sad turn.

I was upset and scared to see our lives turned upside down. Steve just plowed through. He refused to feel bad or be a victim.

I couldn't plow through. I felt guilty. No one should feel guilty when they're shaken by disease or potential loss of a loved one. I shouldn't have felt guilty. You shouldn't either.

As time went on, I finally allowed myself to be upset.

After some soul-searching I realized my guilt was okay. It meant I had built a great love and respect for Steve. The great strength he brought to his life and the self-lessness he showed trickled down, and, while I never took these things for granted, cancer made me face loss head-on.

Life will bring change again. That's a given. This episode prepared me for whatever the future throws my way. Thanks to Steve's love and support, I believe I'll be able to handle the next challenge better.

— David Dubois, Jr.

Cam, now nineteen years old, is one of my four grandkids, known fondly as my Stinky Brats.

I didn't know what to do when Dad came home with news of Grampa's cancer. None of us did.

Losing Grampa wasn't thinkable.

My twin sister Chloe and I have some of our fondest memories with Grampa. Every Saturday, we spent the day with him and learned something new. He was a fountain of knowledge and we were little sponges, eager to soak up his knowledge. He taught me many things I will use for the rest of my life and helped shape me into who I am.

I vividly remember coming home from my driving lesson in 2018 and hearing the news that Grampa Steve was in the hospital. I was in shock. I did not know the seriousness of the brain tumor at first, but once I learned it, I thought to myself, How could this happen? He was only sixty-three and one of the healthiest people I knew. I realized that cancer does not care; anyone of any age can be a victim.

I remember visiting Grampa Steve in the hospital where he sat me down and told me he could die, but we as a family were going to get through it. I knew he would put up a fight and not let cancer get the best of him. Every time I saw Grampa in the hospital, no matter how much I cried (which I did) he stayed positive. Which changed my outlook on life.

Grampa continues to teach me many life lessons that most people do not have the opportunity to learn. One in particular is: every one of us will have difficult situations to deal with, and while we may not always have control of the outcome, we can control how we handle the situation.

Life is too short to make a bad situation worse; all we can do is handle the situation as best we can and try to make it better.

— Cam Costa

I'm so grateful to have a granddaughter as sweet and as caring as my darling Chloe.

When big moments—good or bad—happen to you in life, you always remember exactly where you were and exactly how it played out. Everyone knows exactly where they were when 9/11 happened; ask anyone who was alive during the time. I was not alive, but I have had moments like that. I remember exactly where I was during the Boston Marathon bombing.

Those are wide-scale events. On a more personal level, I remember exactly where I was and what I was doing when my parents told me my grandmother was dying of cancer. I remember exactly what I was doing and where I was when my mother told me she had breast cancer. And I remember the exact moment my parents told me my Grampa Steve had brain cancer. In moments like those, your heart drops. The world around you suddenly stops, and it is all you can think about.

May was a busy month: sophomore year. My finals and driver's test were around the corner. My mother told me she and my father had news to tell us, but we needed to wait until my brother got home. I remember being excited, thinking maybe it was news of a trip for the summer. When my brother came back, we all met in the kitchen. The news was the opposite of exciting. My grandfather had brain cancer.

I had been faced with cancer news before, but I was younger. I was told when things were pretty severe, usually a while after everyone else knew: I did not know my grandmother had breast cancer until it had already spread to her entire body and she was dying. I did not know my mother had breast cancer until she had already made the appointment to get surgery to try to remove it. This was the very beginning of a story that was going to take a lot of mental and physical toughness to get through. This time, I was able to be by my grandfather for the whole ride.

I remember the beginning, when the whole family had first gone to see my grandfather in the hospital. My brother and I were told to go on a walk while my grandfather talked with all the adults. When we got back, the room was not how we left it. Everyone's eyes were red and puffy. I knew immediately something was wrong. Things were severe, and the odds were not in his favor. My grandfather talked to my brother and me about how he—and we as a family—would try to get through this. We cried, and it was the first time in my entire life I had ever seen my grandmother cry. In that moment, I could not think of anything else besides my father. He had already lost his mother to cancer. I really did not think he would be able to make it if he had lost his father to it, too. He has told me before he still remembers vividly what it sounded like when she was dying, her struggling to breathe. He sat with her for hours, listening, until it ceased. I did not want him to have to go through that again.

In the following months, we spent time with my grandfather in the hospital, multiple times a week. I was very behind in school and failed one of my finals, but I did not care. School was the least of my worries. When my grandfather was going through treatment, I slowly saw him drift away from his normal self. Grampa has always been the big boss, literally and figuratively. He is always teaching us lessons, working all the time, occasionally yelling at Cam, and just all-around a figure I look up to. Seeing him slowly slipping terrified me, but I knew I needed to be by his side. Even at his worst, he stayed positive, and we all had hope. I believe his strength, the strength of our small family, and, of course, Dana-Farber, are what got him through this.

— Chloe Costa

I'm blessed by my spirited, precocious, and lovely granddaughter Elle.

I love my Grampa so much. He teaches me to do things no one else would dream of. We climbed a giant eighty-foot-tall sand pile on a construction site and slid down on our bellies. As I write, my head is filled with memories.

One day we were discussing the way we eat and before you knew it, Grampa and I were eating ice cream off of our bellies. It was so crazy and fun.

Before Grampa's cancer, he and I wrote a book together: *The Fox Who Sneezed: Can You Guess What Came Out?*

When Grampa was diagnosed with cancer, I was devastated and didn't want to put our relationship on pause. I thought, "What if it's not a pause but the end?" It made me very upset. I didn't know what to do. I was only eight years old.

When my family and I went to the hospital to visit Grampa, he was the same. He hadn't changed. Grampa, my brother, and I took a walk with his new friend, the solution hanger pole. We named the pole Joe at first, and then a girl's name, too. We ran down the hospital corridor with Joe, the chemicals trailing behind us, saying, "Not running, not running, not running."

People we passed said, "Slow down."

We laughed, slowed down a little bit, and repeated, "Not running."

Cancer didn't change Grampa one bit!

Now I'm almost eleven, but even at eight I knew I wasn't done learning from Grampa. I am happy he is alive. I'm proud to have a Grampa like him. I can't explain it to people. Grampa is one of the happiest influences in my life. I feel like I escape everything when I'm with him. I can just be myself. I love him to the moon and back.

Sometimes I don't want to escape the bad stuff with Grampa. We talk about the bad stuff and then it doesn't seem so bad. I love all the stories Grampa tells ranging from burning fires to cupcakes. Thanks for listening to my side of the story.

I love my Grampa so much and he knows it. *Cancer R.I.P.!*

— Elle Valentina Dubois

My gratitude is bottomless for my independent but irascible grandson D3.

I'm David Dubois the III, so Grampa calls me D3 ... and Stinky Brat. When I found out about his cancer, I was scared. I was only five, but I noticed lots of whispering at dinnertime. I guess I wasn't supposed to know about it.

I didn't know what it was, but I heard "cansa" a lot and figure it was something important. When Grampa went to the hospital, I wondered if he and I would ever ride bikes together again.

I knew Grampa wasn't going to die, but while I was thinking that, I worried that he was going to die. It was strange to have him in the hospital instead of at home with us.

After his stem cell operation, Grampa sat down with me and tried to explain cansa. He said something stopped his brain from working. He lost his balance, too.

We did ride bikes again, but Grampa was slower than before. We got lost a lot but it was okay. He came home.

— D3, David Dubois III

My best friend Luis planted himself at my side for the ride of our lifetimes.

Steve and I had been best friends for five years before cancer hit. Even so, I didn't realize how much we meant to each other until I got the news. It's a guy thing, I guess. We had each other's back. We'd do favors for each other. Whatever was asked was granted, and not too much was asked. We just liked each other and enjoyed beating the hell out of our bodies together on early-morning runs and bike rides.

I was devastated when Steve called with the news. He was a mess, too. He was all over the place. His speech wasn't typical. His thoughts were disorganized.

In our first conversation about his condition, he talked about his kids, his insurance, his bike, his cancer … all in one live-streamed breath. I quickly realized how much trouble he was in.

At work, I run a good-sized food plant, always busy with tons of responsibility. Yet somehow, I had always shoe-horned our weekly bike rides or a jog with Steve into my schedule.

Now, I knew I had to step up. I told my boss I needed time off and went straight to the hospital to sit with Steve and his family. I told him I would do anything he, his wife, or his kids needed.

This was a crap deal for Steve, who was always looking out for others. I hoped I could help him now.

Here are some things I'd like you to know if this happens to your best friend:

1.Your job can wait. This is the now-or-never time to help out.

2.Find the right balance to be with your friend without taking away precious time from his family.

3.I could tell his kids, Dave and Phil, whom I knew well, needed a steady voice. I focused on being that voice.

— Luis Tueme

How lucky I am to have a tough-as-nails, devoted, and beautiful wife forever at my side.

My life was going along just fine with my wonderful husband, children, grandchildren, family, friends, pets, work, vacations, etc. Busy, busy, busy, always rushing. Little did I know a bomb was about to go off.

As most years did, 2018 began with a family meeting about each member's goals for the upcoming months. I wanted to play piano, get a new job, spend Thanksgiving at our Florida home, and have a garden. A family medical crisis wasn't on my goals list, but I got one.

In May, Steve started getting lost and forgetful; he was losing his eyesight. We knew something was wrong and told our immediate family on May 31 that we would be going to the hospital the next morning. Steve's son asked me what could be wrong.

"Well, I don't think he had a stroke, or an infection, and it doesn't seem like an electrolyte imbalance," I said. "The only thing left is a brain tumor, but how likely is that?"

On June 1, I found out my husband had a large mass in his head. On June 2 we learned the mass was a tumor the size of an avocado. On June 5, we found out he had central nervous system (CNS) lymphoma. In a blink of our eyes, our lives exploded.

CNS lymphoma is a form of diffuse B-cell non-Hodgkin's lymphoma. The incidence of CNS is about three in a million people. It has a dismally low rate of eradication and a high rate of recurrence.

In a few short days, I ground through the five stages of grief and loss.

First were denial and isolation: I made up my mind I was only going to tell a few people about this, and no one at work. I wanted work to be a place I didn't have to talk about this mess.

Next came anger: I couldn't accept that I was going to lose Steve so soon. I was good at anger, but it didn't last long. The pace of Steve's disease ripped time away from us. I had to act fast. Time is brain, in this case.

Bargaining and depression: I skipped these stages. There was no time for them. Although I often cried, mostly around my son and his family, I knew crying and being depressed wouldn't help me.

At some point I cannot clearly recall, I accepted that we were stuck with this and we had better get on board with the diagnosis and treatment, or it would be too late. It was full speed ahead.

Chapter 24

I seized every opportunity to learn more, do more, and be more aware of everything that was going on, good or bad.

Being a physician assistant for twenty years was both a blessing and a curse. A blessing because I understood most of what was happening and going to happen, and a curse because I understood most of what was happening and going to happen.

I also knew my husband and I knew myself. I knew Steve wasn't going down without a fight if we could help it.

I pulled myself together using all of my strengths: being organized, speaking with the staff, making sure Steve did what was required. He needed to move forward with the horrible treatments. I kept a notebook, a calendar, and a journal, which helped me with the organization and scheduling.

As I always do with my patients, I read about CNS lymphoma, its characteristics, treatments, dismal prognosis, and how frightening the disease was. I sent updates to his family almost every day; sometimes I hated to give bad news, but I knew if I were in their shoes, I would want to know what was going on.

The one person I usually could confide in was Steve. But this time he couldn't help me. He didn't really know what was going on, even though he was the person most affected.

He seemed distant and non-reactive to the constant changes in treatments and plans. The emotional swings from those changes wrecked me.

Steve missed the emotional swings, the day-to-day highs and lows of the diagnosis, treatments, and procedures. He was mentally out of it.

Infuriating mistakes were made. Steve couldn't comprehend the importance of the information I received daily. As a medical professional, I knew too much. I had trouble holding back my anger.

My friend Becky always said, "What would Jackie Onassis do?"

Would she scream, or cry, or act like an ostrich with her head in the sand? No, she would always lead with courage and grace. I tried to be brave, strong, and effective. It probably doesn't make sense, but that was my mantra.

I tried to be positive around Steve, even though some days the news was disappointing, and I could tell he didn't understand the full implications of the new information.

I spent a lot of time on the road, driving by myself. Most days I drove forty miles to and from work. After work, I drove another forty traffic-bound minutes to and from the hospital in Boston. It was exhausting and lonely.

During these alone times, I sometimes thought about the worst: How were we going to get through this, if we ever could? What was it going to take? Was Steve going to die? Did I have the stamina to help myself and my family through?

I knew Steve did. Initially as a distraction in my car time, I started listening to the words of the songs on the radio. I wrote down any titles that inspired me or made me think about the funeral that might be coming up.

Ariana Grande's "Breathin"—Time goes by and I can't control my mind. Don't know what else to try, but you tell me every time—Just keep breathin' and breathin' and breathin' and breathin.

Chapter 24

Or Shawn Mendes's "In My Blood"—I need somebody now, someone to help me out. I need somebody now. Help me, it's like the walls are caving in. Sometimes I feel like giving up, but I just can't. It isn't in my blood.

Work was hard, too. There was so much work and no time to talk. Work was stressful, and my personal stress didn't help the situation. I took care of very sick people, some with cancer, some with brain injuries, all with serious problems that reminded me of our predicament and what a terrible outcome could be headed our way.

I didn't want to hear coworkers' stories about who had what kind of cancer, who lived, and who died. I wanted someone to tell me our nightmare would have a happy ending, and no one anywhere could help me with that.

Sleeping was tough. Sometimes I was tired enough to sleep, but most times I had trouble. The first night at home alone, I woke with a start. I thought I had a nightmare. It took me a few minutes of sitting up in bed to realize this wasn't a nightmare. It was real!

My new reality was hard to accept. The man I loved, who loved me, whom I had planned to retire and grow old with, was going to die at the young age of sixty-three, and I couldn't stop the speeding train that was sending us down the tracks to his death. I felt helpless and hopeless sometimes, but then his wonderfully positive attitude would temporarily right the ship and steer us to a happy place of hope.

Neither of us had any idea what was ahead: the grueling hospitalizations, the chemotherapy, the many moments when he was not lucid and seemed to have lost his mind and memory. The long hours in the hospital, the waits for test results, the many MRIs, CT scans, ultrasounds, X-rays, medications ....

I was with him every step of the way. It might have been easier to go through it myself than to watch it happen to Steve. Sometimes I had to call the family for backup because I couldn't spend another minute in that hospital room.

We didn't know if Steve would survive. Not knowing was the worst, so much uncertainly, so many unanswerable questions, such vast, uncharted territory. There seemed to be unending changes in plans and treatments, with complications and a constant piling on of more problems and more issues. The unknowns were hard, but sometimes the known seemed worse than the unknown.

The pain of watching someone you love fading away is horrible. I still can't fathom how I made it through— never mind how Steve did. It seemed like I was just a bystander who could do nothing to help.

I could only remember what came before. Every single thing in our lives changed. I just remember every day saying to myself, "Just keep breathin'. Just put one foot in front of the other and go out the door and handle whatever comes. You can do it. You're going to get through it."

Somehow I got to the other end of the crisis, not really knowing how I got here. It took forever to feel better about things.

Funnily enough, I could never have done it without Steve's positive outlook. Even facing death, he was able to make his family and friends feel like he had just received the opportunity of a lifetime. This experience has changed the course of all our lives.

Some things I think everyone should know:

Keep your family and close friends in the loop. Confide in them and let them help you when they can. You need them and they need you. It helps everyone feel better and more useful.

Take a lot of notes! You won't remember anything that any physician or anyone else tells you. It's too confusing, and you're too upset to receive information and process it correctly. Steve wasn't much help remembering anything either.

Most importantly, this ongoing saga has reminded me that time is all we have. Remember this! I have constantly been reminded that money-fame-work-careers-possessions don't matter at all.

Many things I thought were important were not. Time is all there is. Don't squander time. You're not getting it back. Make sure you say what you want to say and do what you want to do while you can.

Tell everyone important to you that you love them. And mean it. I once saw a sign that said: Don't look back; you're not going that way! So true, and yet we are always worrying about what happened in the past or what's going to happen next.

When the CNS lymphoma bomb hit, we never saw it coming. Nothing that we could have done would have ever prepared us for what was coming. We cannot predict the future.

Now I know what is worth worrying about. And—unless it's brain cancer—it's probably not that important.

— Susan DeBalsi

Lessons Learned

- Those who love you, really love you, stay by your side in the worst of times.
- Live your life to impact others and future generations.
- Children can surprise you with their capacity to understand (and withstand) serious situations.
- Hold tight to those you love.

Questions Begging Answers

- Can I ever repay those loved ones who sacrificed so much in my behalf?
- Will I, in their hours of need, be present for friends and family? (I hope so, and I intend to!)

BONUS DAYS

Roused by chirping sounds so bright,
  morning bids the moon goodnight.
Eyes stretch and blink, salute the sun;
  my stem cell transplant work is done.
Sunrise—such a welcome sight,
  these extra hours worth the fight.
Sunrays spread their warmth so free
  as Cancer Rests in Peace with me.

My heart and soul are filled with light
  by bonus days and bonus nights.
Chemo pushed the end away,
  a lucky ticket yet to play.
Nurses, doctors, PAs, too,
  toiled together, were the glue.
With friends and family holding true,
  I'm free to roam, to love anew.

Chakra shivers through my spine;
  my family's hopes and prayers align.
Like butterflies, so free and lithe,
  I fly to embrace a hopeful life.

—STEVE KELLEY

ACKNOWLEDGMENTS

My deepest appreciation is for my family—true saints, angels, and heroes in my life—along with my KC team, Lisa Flashenburg and Gaby Tueme. How lucky I am!

Thank you to my doctors and nurses, PAs, unseen researchers, aides, and other medical professionals who helped me traverse a trail I never imagined riding. Dr. Yaakov Weinreb, Dr. Andrew Kriegel, Dr. Mazen Eneyni, Dr. Lakshmi Nayak, Dr. Timothy Smith, and Dr. Ann LaCasce all deserve special recognition for the roles they played in my cancer journey—from diagnosis through treatment.

I also extend sincere thanks to my mountain biking team, who became an important part of my recovery: Luis, Shawn, Luke, Gary, Fast Rob, Chowe, Zoe, Harley, Drew, Anthony, Dave R., Guy, Manny, Joe, Chris, Matt, Mark, Matty, Kevin, Mark, and the whole Bike Barn team.

I offer sincere gratitude to my book team: Carol McAdoo Rehme, Meredith Dunn, Charissa and Robert Newell, Trina Kaye, Dez Savoy, Serena Finocchio, and MaryEllen O'Rourke at our great printers, A&A printing in Tampa, Florida.

ACKNOWLEDGMENTS

We all need supporters, and mine are exceptional: long-time friends Linda and Edmund Ostrander, Jorge Cardoso, Joe Feaster, Ken Ryvicker, Pat and Jerry Gautreau, Alan Lury, Becky and Dennis Devlin, Sam Reef, Bob Mendillo, Sarah Feragen, Brooks Winchell, Eric Dias, David Wluka, Mark Joyce, James, Yola, and Sophie Thorp.

ABOUT THE
AUTHOR

Steve Kelley is a successful entrepreneur, real estate developer, professor, and personal coach. He is also a writer, triathlete, public speaker, local talk show host, and volunteer extraordinaire.

Steve overcame a devastating, inoperable brain tumor—primary central nervous system lymphoma—and a radical stem cell transplant in 2018-2019.

Just five months after his hospitalization, Steve and his wife, Susan, a physician assistant, celebrated his recovery by traveling to Italy to see her grandparents' homeland. They joined a biking group, which followed the Giro D'Italia Tour race trail.

Steve's new memoir, *Cancer R.I.P.: The Ultimate Fight*, details his inspirational success story—including the vast lessons he learned and the overwhelming questions he faced. His miracle recovery models confidence and strength to fight life's demons.

In 2020, Steve released *Break the Curse: A Template for Change*, a self-help book. In 2017, he and his granddaughter, Elle Dubois, coauthored *The Fox Who Sneezed*.

Steve lives in Sharon, Massachusetts, in a multi-generational home of his own design that he shares with his wife, kids, and grandkids. Their proximity to Borderland State Park allows him to follow his avocation of mountain biking. He rides with his team of biking buddies "in all weathers," five days a week.

Other hobbies include triathlons, breakdancing, summer ice fishing, and withstanding MRIs every three months. Steve's armament for life includes a good sense of humor that ensures he can always be the delicate flower he was meant to be.

Also by Steve Kelley:

BREAK THE CURSE

A TEMPLATE FOR CHANGE

10 Steps to Restart Your Life

For more from Freedom Press:

WWW.FREEDOMPRESS.ORG

For more from One Stop Publishing :

WWW.ONESTOPPUBLISHING.COM

One Stop
PUBLISHING